The Empire Sells Out

First published in Australia in 2021
by Guy Morgan #guymorganartist

Written and illustrated by Guy Morgan
PO Box 4037, Castlecrag NSW 2068
(guy@guymorgan.com)

Cover design by Gemma Banks
Book design by Gemma Banks

Proofreading by Susan McCreery

Printed and bound in Australia
by IngramSpark/Lightning Source Australia

A catalogue record for this book is available from the National Library of Australia.

ISBN 978-0-6453017-0-0 (hardback)
ISBN 978-0-6453017-1-7 (paperback)
ISBN 978-0-6453017-2-4 (ebook)

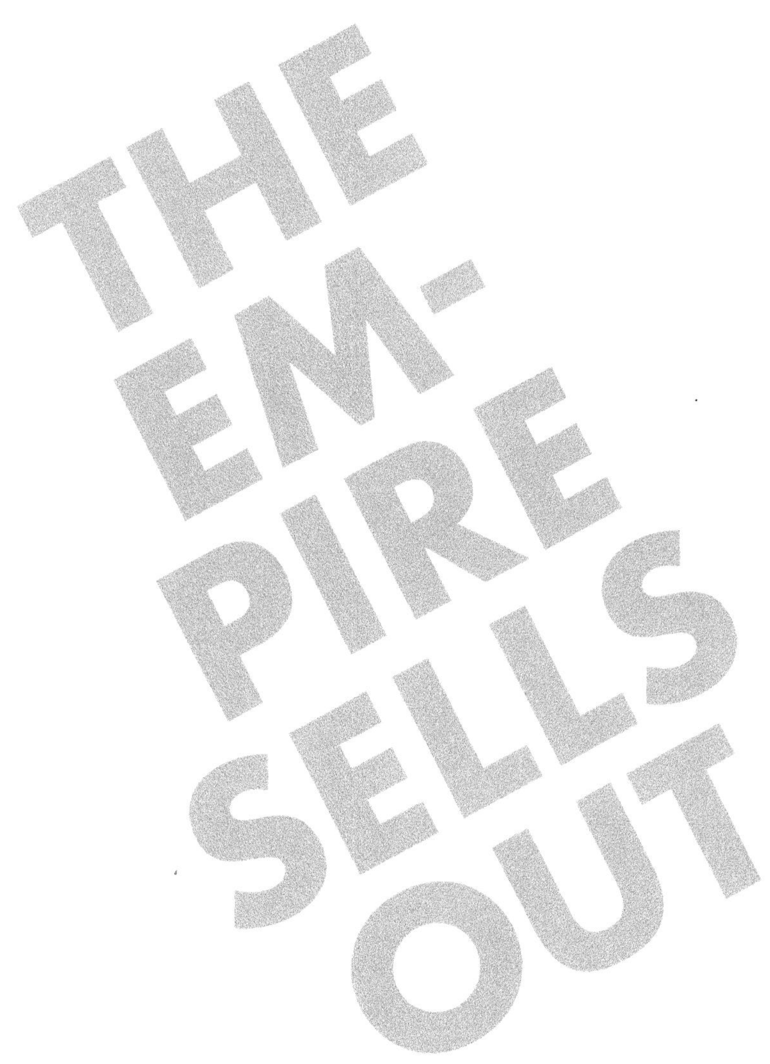

Written and illustrated by
Guy Morgan

For Fiona and Max, Kevin C, Rob E & Gary D.
And Gladys.

6 Foreword
8 The Emperor
15 Figures of Speech
19 The Empire – The 'Official' Version
20 The Empire – In Actuality
23 Out of the City
28 The Art World Is Rapidly Descending
36 Growing Up
40 Interested Parties
44 Times Change
48 Clear the Air
52 A Little Insight
56 Lack of Common Decency
59 Look at It This Way
63 Lies and Deceit
64 Surveillance
68 The Emperor's Retreat
75 Letters to the Editor
76 Fun and Games
80 Working and Not Working Relationships
83 Mistaken Identity
87 The Epilogue (Before Its Time)
91 Excuse Me, Emperor
100 By Way of Explanation
103 Appendix – The Illustrations

Foreword

This book is part social commentary, part fiction, concentrating on current society, the media and issues concerning celebrity, art, ambition, exclusion and accessibility.

It presents a series of light-hearted observations concerning issues with which readers readily identify. The narrative touches on unwanted leadership, the pressure of fame, the struggle in forming meaningful relationships, the desire to attain anonymity and the sometimes difficult process of succession.

Accompanying 48 illustrations (there's a section on these at the back of this book), this tale includes various elements of the nature of our changing culture and the diversity of reactions to daily issues. I'll address what is achievable, what is not, what it's like to stand in others' shoes, and I'll speculate about what may come next. This work proves that we are not alone in forming the attitudes or the positions we choose – hopefully eliciting the quiet response 'that's true'.

Topics include outsider elements, disability and other social inequities such as ageism.

I also want to make you laugh (preferably out loud) at the ridiculousness of life.

This book is a major step in my career development – extending my output as an artist, illustrator, curator, teacher, writer and gallerist – reaching out to new and wider audiences. Writing this book will also be a pathway to gaining literary representation and a publishing company in due course. (I hope!)

In the short term, I will use my website, www.guymorgan.com, together with my social media presence, #guymorganartist, and word of mouth (please spread the word, not the virus), to promote the book. I will also look for PR opportunities and distribute press releases to news outlets, book and art publications and websites. In the future, and as a separate exercise, as venues become more accessible (post-Covid), I will market and write proposals to stage art exhibitions of the illustrations in selected regional, municipal and commercial galleries, and other venues in NSW, Australia, around the World and across the Empire. I'll also sell the original paintings and produce limited edition fine art prints. Basically, I'll do anything to make a buck. You are also welcome to contact me via guy@guymorgan.com

I don't expect fame or fortune but will aim the work at individuals, collectors, book retailers, online outlets, gallery/gallery shops and various other types of mug punters.

At this point, I'd like to thank NSW Government and particularly Create NSW for their valuable support.

What is the focused engagement offered to Aboriginal people through this project?

The identification of social inequities – how not all are treated in the same way or with the same benefits of birthright.

What is the focused engagement offered to people with a CaLD background through this project?

The narrative is not based in a single country but a universal state.

What is the focused engagement offered to people living/working in regional NSW through this project?

Every citizen should have the same access to services and transport.

What is the focused engagement offered to people living/working in Western Sydney through this project?

The world does not revolve purely around decisions made in the capital.

What is the focused engagement offered to people with disability through this project?

Universal access is everyone's right. The author is disabled.

What is the focused engagement offered to young people through this project?

Young people are the future and their opinion matters. They are tomorrow's leaders.

So, onwards and upwards...

#theempiresellsout

– Guy Morgan, Sydney 2020/21

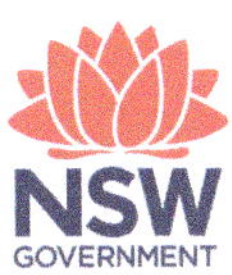

This project is supported by the NSW Government through Create NSW.

'I'm the voice and sometimes interruption in your head,' said Narrator. 'You will always know it's me; I'm just "here". Think of me as your personal guide to the Empire! When I have something *especially important to say, I'll occasionally be in italics…* and at other times, I won't. Now listen up.'

Closely guarding his privacy, the Emperor is not happy in his role and senses the position forced upon him. Was it an accident of birth or some darker conspiracy?

Having ascended to the job, the Emperor was only too aware of the precariousness of his elevated position.

Notwithstanding, it's essential the Emperor remains 'top of mind' across the Empire. In these turbulent times omnipotent leadership is expected.

Hoping to see the storyline – or at least a happy conclusion on the horizon – he decided to put the prequel behind him.

The Emperor is a hard man to pin down. Citizens generally admire him across the Empire as a good leader – the one who makes decisions no one else can, with outcomes aimed at benefiting society.

Being on top was especially difficult for this shy recluse and he was acutely aware there were those who wanted him out.

Unconventionally, perhaps, he was highly sympathetic to their cause.

Despite his popularity, his security detail takes no risks when it comes to his personal safety. They make sure he is never seen in public – or, more precisely, recognised. The result is, the Emperor never appears in the paparazzi's long lenses. It is also impossible for him to be shanghaied by opportunists (or other ne'er-do-wells), and aspirant assassins never know when or in which direction to point their weapons or whom to aim them at.

The lack of newsworthy (or not so worthy) pictures in the media is also due to the Emperor's reticence for self-promotion.

The Emperor feels isolated, not in a bad way, as it goes 'with the territory'. His biographer puts it down to an unusual upbringing, with no family to speak of other than the Emperor Mother.

The story goes that his parents divorced when he was very young and then his father died. The Emperor has no memory of the turmoil. His Mother remarried but wasn't very good at pretending to be a conventional, contented wife – she frequently suffered from downheartedness and it can be difficult, when from the moment you wake, you wish you hadn't.

The second consort of the Emperor Mother only rates a mention because he enjoyed pushing around and intimidating the staff. He couldn't bear to be in the company of anyone who demonstrated more power or influence than he.

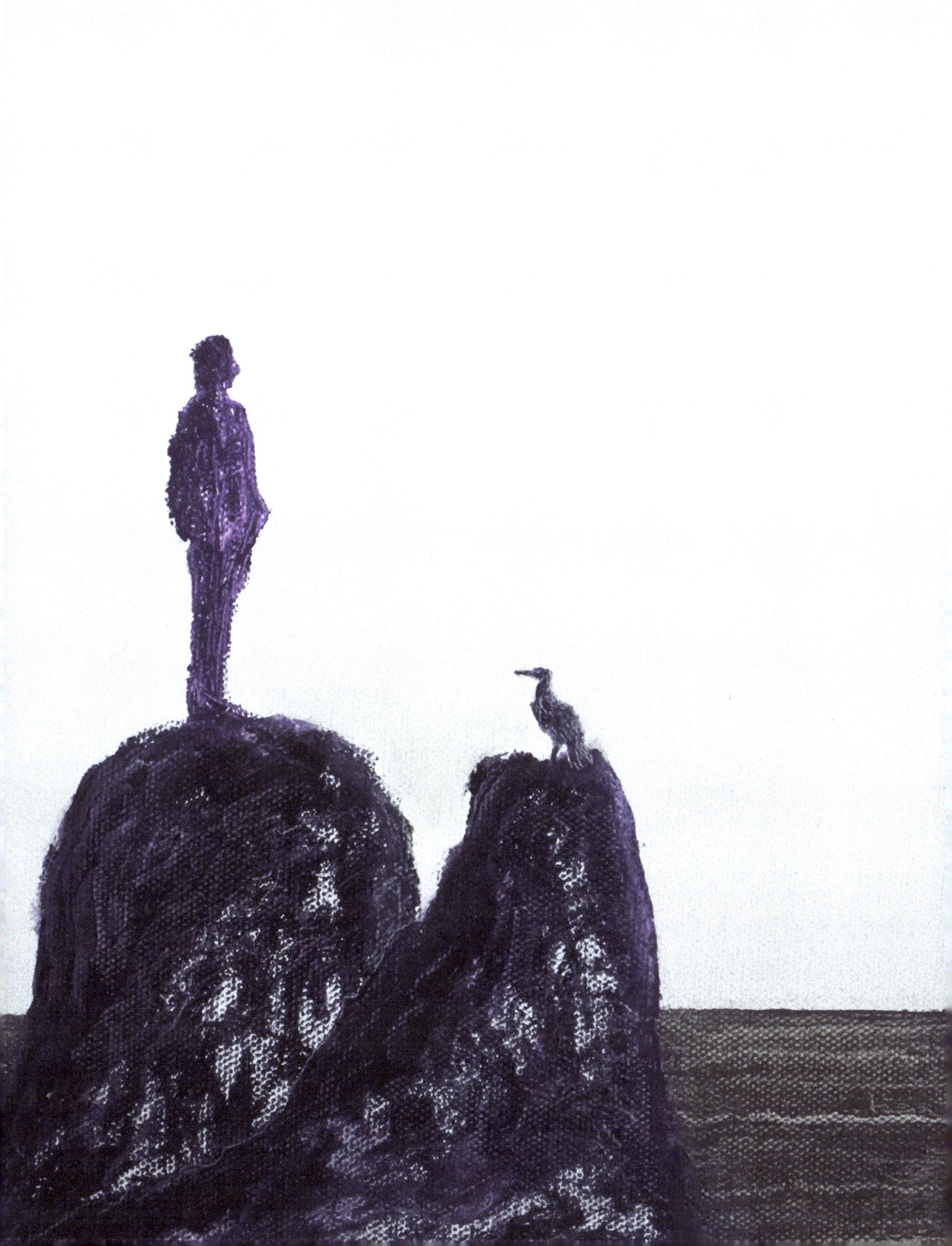

Isolated by power, the Emperor was a good man (but not always). Occasionally, people called him two-faced (but never to his face) because no one really knew what he looked like, and he liked it that way.

Happiest with a ball at his feet or riding his non-thoroughbred horse (the Emperor hated the class system), he was a man of simple tastes.

In short, the Emperor was utterly unsuited to his position as leader of the subjugated worlds and hated the way everyone looked up to him.

As a result and being an 'only child', the Emperor did not have the joyful start in life normally expected in 'privileged society'. Public servants were brought in to try and 'jolly the household along' (professionally of course), but with little success. It made no sense that the Emperor should have to put up with a father figure anyway – particularly one with a power problem. Wanting to expunge his stepfather from his thoughts, daily life and the (official) record, the Emperor acquired a series of meaningful surrogate 'dads'.

The list of notables who have gone publicly unacknowledged until now started with the local (that's 'local' not 'lo-cal') milkman (Mr Crate), who gave the Emperor his first job at the age of four. This was in the days of daily milk deliveries to every street. Someone in the dairy head office thought of expanding the service to include butter, and before long the revolutionary idea of adding yoghurt to the 'float' gained traction. The death knell was trying to introduce fruit juice to the service, the thought of which was well and truly blood-curdling to the average conservative consumer. The Emperor could see the end coming. Shortly after turning 12, he left the daily round and put the previously enjoyable early morning starts behind him.

If he'd stayed on another 17 years, he might have received a precious metal-plated watch.

The handyman (Mr Mason) followed a year or two later, teaching him how to work wood, how to be 'good with his hands' and take very long tea breaks.

The artist (JR) inspired the Emperor throughout his formative teen years and tried to teach him the finer points of playing lawn bowls – particularly when there was no lawn as such – carefully outlining the use of bias in hilly terrain. A physicist or landscape gardener might have been more effective, but the experience became useful in deflecting journalistic criticism in later years.

The little-known fact that the young Emperor was effectively colour blind – in the red/green spectrum – may also have restricted his abilities, thereby avoiding possible opprobrium both artistic-wise and lawn bowl-wise.

Another memorable, if ineffective, influence was the barefoot Maths professor (Mr Manon), who spectacularly failed to share the secrets of calculus (even though he tried hard[2]), but being a long-haired hippy from the 60s' Western bloc of the USA (United Smokers' Association), he was more than happy to share his knowledge of the finer points of various illicit substances with his young charge.

The Emperor Mother (EM) appellation stemmed from a common trait whereby accurate usage of the apostrophe proved impossible.

So as not to get it wrong, the offending article's usage was outlawed when referring to any member of the household.

EM didn't live cocooned in a remote crystal palace.

It was in Reality, in a charming, two-bedroom semi, located in the Easterly Suburbs (naturally).

The neighbours rallied round and were supportive, but it was not remotely private. From time to time, and despite her security detail (headed up by General Direction), the paparazzi would point their lenses at her shutters to see what was up in her darkened rooms.

No one ever remembered seeing her son.

From a young age, the Emperor had difficulty in getting to sleep. It seemed a destination his daily itinerary somehow lacked. His mind never switched off.

The good thing about being an insomniac is that there are more thinking hours – which is fine in daylight, but at night-time any normal person looks for downtime, combined with shut-eye and the off-switch.

Not that there was anything normal about the Emperor.

Occasionally, in semi-sleep, his thoughts would truly roam, leaving him in a state of euphoria. When he came to, he felt he'd missed out, because a large proportion of the day seemed to have disappeared, leaving little time to attend to many pressing matters.

He didn't like the trade-off.

Growing up fast, the Emperor had more than made do. Gaining knowledge outside the classroom environment made him adaptable, highly resourceful and left him well positioned for leadership.

However, he had an uneasy feeling that his experience was not unique and the Empire's official education system needed overhauling – while some practitioners needed hauling over the coals.

The Emperor could count the number of naturally good teachers he had encountered through his formal schooling years as fewer than the fingers he had on one hand. He thought if the education system could be fixed, the results would clearly benefit everyone.

The lack of natural teaching ability was often all too obvious. Inadequate financing was usually cited as the major difficulty, but that was only part of the problem. Teachers being worn out and underappreciated made the situation worse.

Some – particularly the Teachers' Assembly – enjoyed the ongoing conflagration, as it provided ample ammunition with which to cane the Emperor.

He began formulating a solution, and with a decided lack of originality he named the policy the 'Clever Empire'.

Another issue was school uniforms.

Adults (and those 'in charge') can be really unkind, thought the Emperor. Making a mental note, he added it to his 'to do' list.

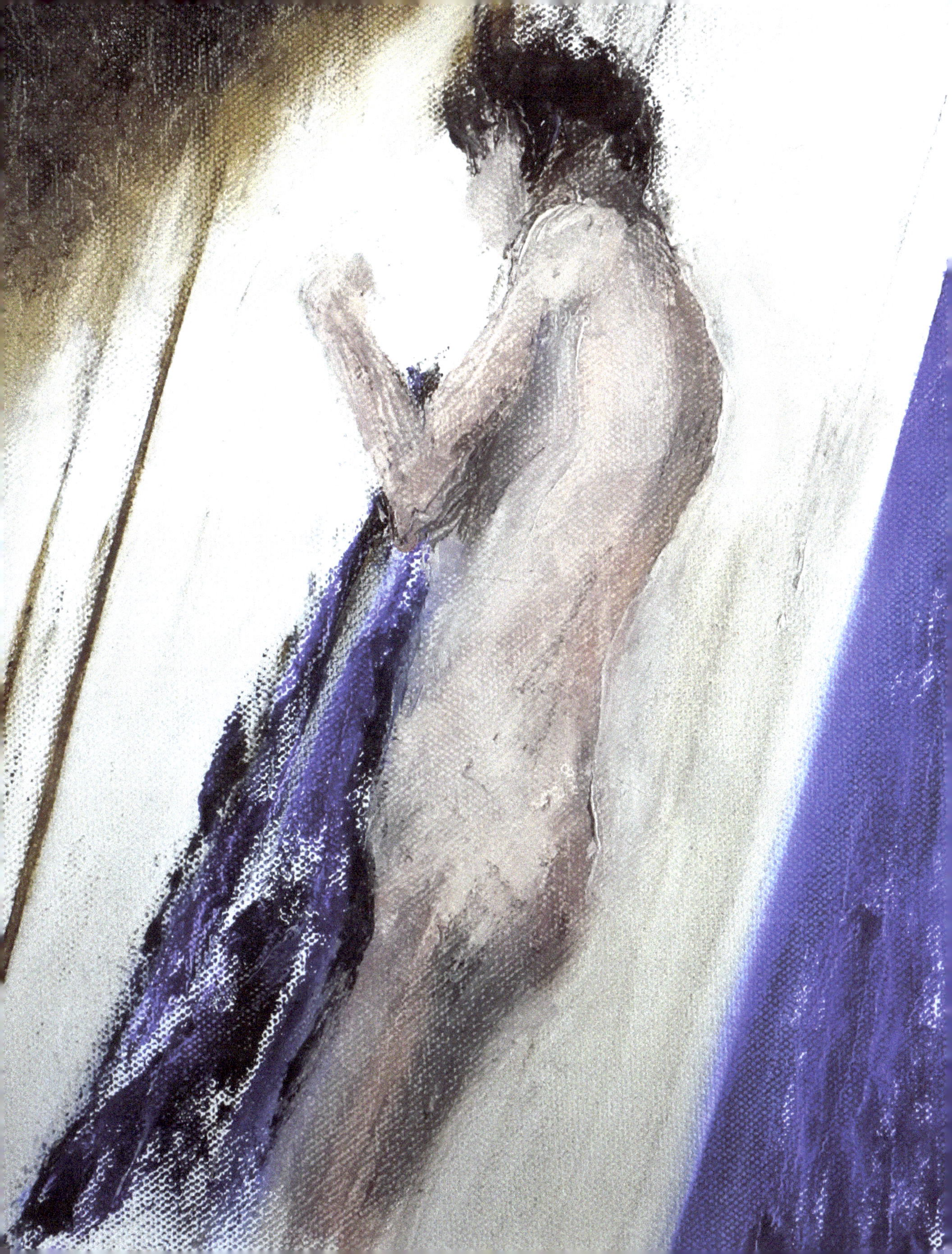

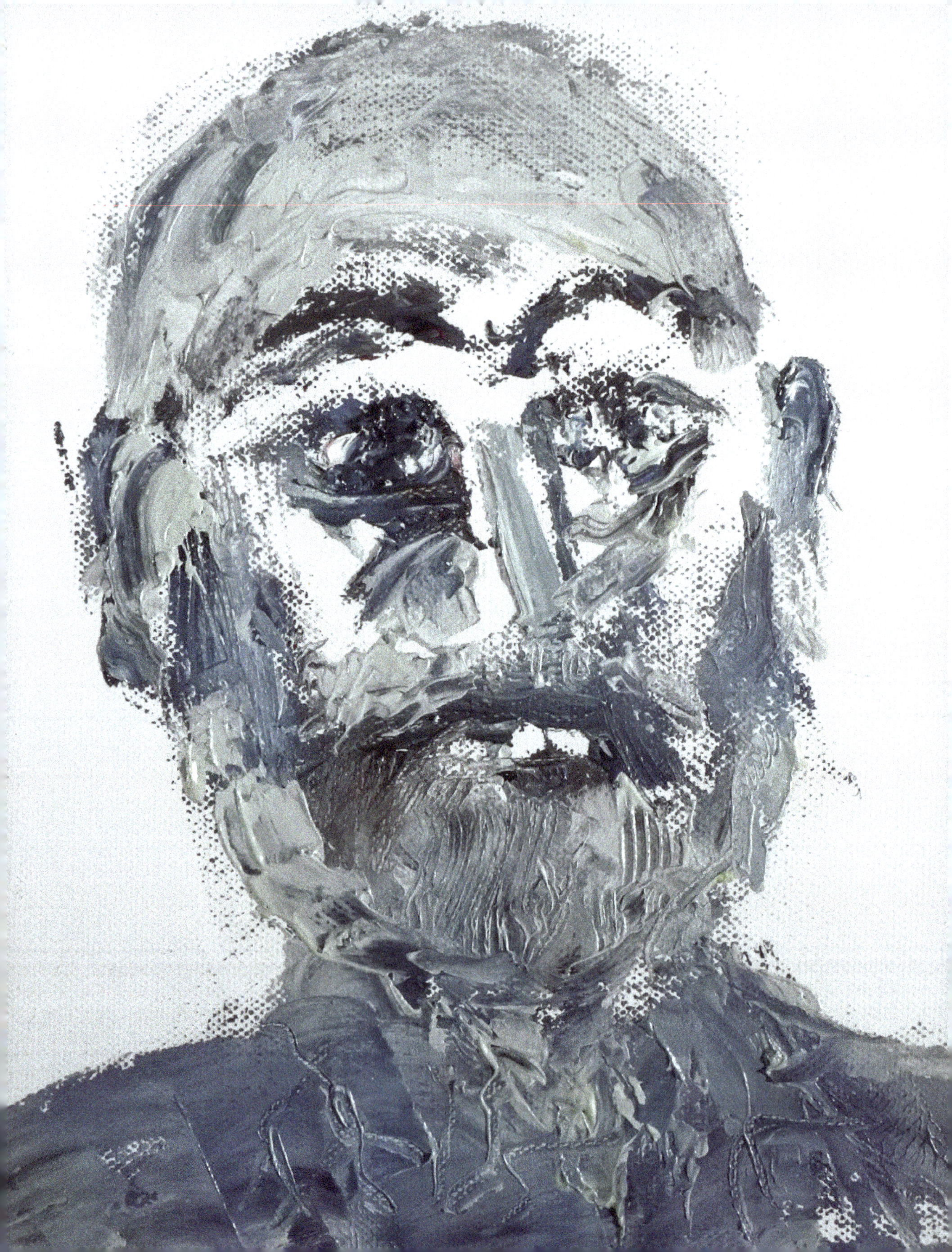

The Emperor spent a great deal of time and energy mentally wrestling with the Dichotomies (about whom, more later). It wasn't just one inconsistency he worried about. There were several contrarieties that weighed heavily on him. It was very hard to find common ground – so many different interests staked their right of legitimacy, claiming sovereignty as traditional owners. If only it was as simple to understand as time, mused the Emperor, unamusedly. Some considered amoebas had ultimate land rights but their banners were hard to read and they had little experience in the art of protesting.

For a couple of reasons, Two-toof was easy to recognise even in the half-light. He was the very model of a Neanderthal half-wit.

A timeless school bully, he had the nickname 'Buck'. Often shouting his usual greeting, 'Take your glasses off, PUN-K!', Two-toof proved to have remarkable foresight.

Optometry hadn't been invented at the time.

The intellectuals' reply of 'Who's Punk?' was followed by a favourite insult that few, if any, understood – 'You mocplete liplock!'

The story goes that the Emperor (like most normal mortals) wasn't suited to the playground, which was Two-toof's domain.

Amazingly, both Two-toof and the Emperor had something in common.

From an early age – and due to different causes – both found it impossible to make friends of any real substance.

'You simply don't know how lucky you are,' blurted Antagonist. 'I'll tell you, MR Emperor, what it means to make your way through the world as an ordinary man, or woman, Aboriginal, linguistically or culturally diverse, rich or poor, based in the regions or living outside the capital, young, old, intellectually, vertically or pigmentally challenged, tall, disabled, visually impaired or blind, hard of hearing or deaf, LGBTQIAU2CV, a dickhead (insert your preferred label here) or, for that matter, any other typical or atypical member of the public, with society's power structures, inherent hierarchy, inequities and in-built oppression – life is tough. You don't know you're born!'

'And you haven't the slightest idea, MR Antagonist,' Retort retorted. 'Try being the effing Emperor!!!'

The Emperor never talked to anyone directly. For him there was a different way of communicating. No good at dialogue and no desire to start a conversation, he was much better at framing thoughts than issuing edicts. He personally didn't make any orders or dispense proclamations...others did that for him, in his name.

A further similarity you may notice with your 'normal' world is the day-to-day mistakes made by those 'in charge'. Truths in the media (conspiracies or fake news), assumptions made by arts world 'leaders', both visual and literary, conceptual bigwigs and those who ask fifteen-minute questions that require a simple 'yes' or 'no' answer, any type of critic or commentator and people who have a far higher view of their importance than warranted are other examples.

That covers a large proportion of the population and, almost certainly, everyone you've noticed in the public eye.

'Ah yes, but the tall poppy syndrome is one of society's ways of levelling the playing field,' replied Retort.

('But oh, were it more effective.'), Mr Bracket added. Mrs Bracket (née Parenthesis) concurred.

Rarely seen but often heard muttering negative comments across the Empire, is Antagonist. (And we all know who that is.)

Antagonist doesn't take sides. He's against everything and everybody and is particularly potent as the Emperor's nemesis.

Pictured in this rare society column scoop from the Tittle-Tattle-Prattle Gazette, Antagonist is surrounded by the Brackets, who feel it their civic duty to stick close by, and, in the name of common decency, attempt to moderate his vile remarks.

Moving in the opposite direction is the ghostly presence of Retort. Her withering observations and biting facetiousness echo in the context.

Even Antagonist knows there can be no escape from true wit.

Antagonist is a curious creature, but then so is his habitat. When asked to describe it, he condescendingly replied, 'You'd find the Empire recognisable but different from anything you've experienced (in your version of reality). There go Brackets adding their moderation, so hopefully you won't feel overly insulted.

Here it's worth mentioning how the Brackets got together (in a manner of speaking).

Interestingly, there are images available (taken by different cameras) of the Brackets standing together with others before they had even opened dialogue (which of course is not what brackets do).

They first met at a rooftop garden party overlooking Mathematics Beach (the complex plane of one of the most clichéd urban coastlines in the Eastern Sea Bored) – on Empire celebration day. Open Bracket had broken up with his previous partner and was moping around as singularities often do.

About to leave alone, his eye was attracted to a bright skirt and, as he puts it, 'a captivating foot of anatomy (30cm)' – a brown knee and calf muscle – a symphonic shape emerging and vanishing, weaving its way through the crowd.

The curvature (and the rest of the shapely assemblage) was observed joining a small set – fronting away from Open. In a desire to see the attached visage, he walked around the gathering to face her, and as he did so, he was recognised by many of the group's components and was instantly invited to join them to be photographed together (rather like parts of speech forming a sentence).

The resulting images (when developed) first showed Open checking out Miss Parenthesis – who was originally from the land of the long white crowd. The second photo, taken at a slightly different angle, shows Open grinning (broadly).

The group dispersed and suddenly the future Brackets were left together, facing each other.

What isn't shown is what happened next.

Over the years, there are consistently a few characters and assorted types that come between them, but as a couple (though not completely inseparable), one will always wait for the other, no matter how long the sentence.

Mr and Mrs Bracket are made to be together.

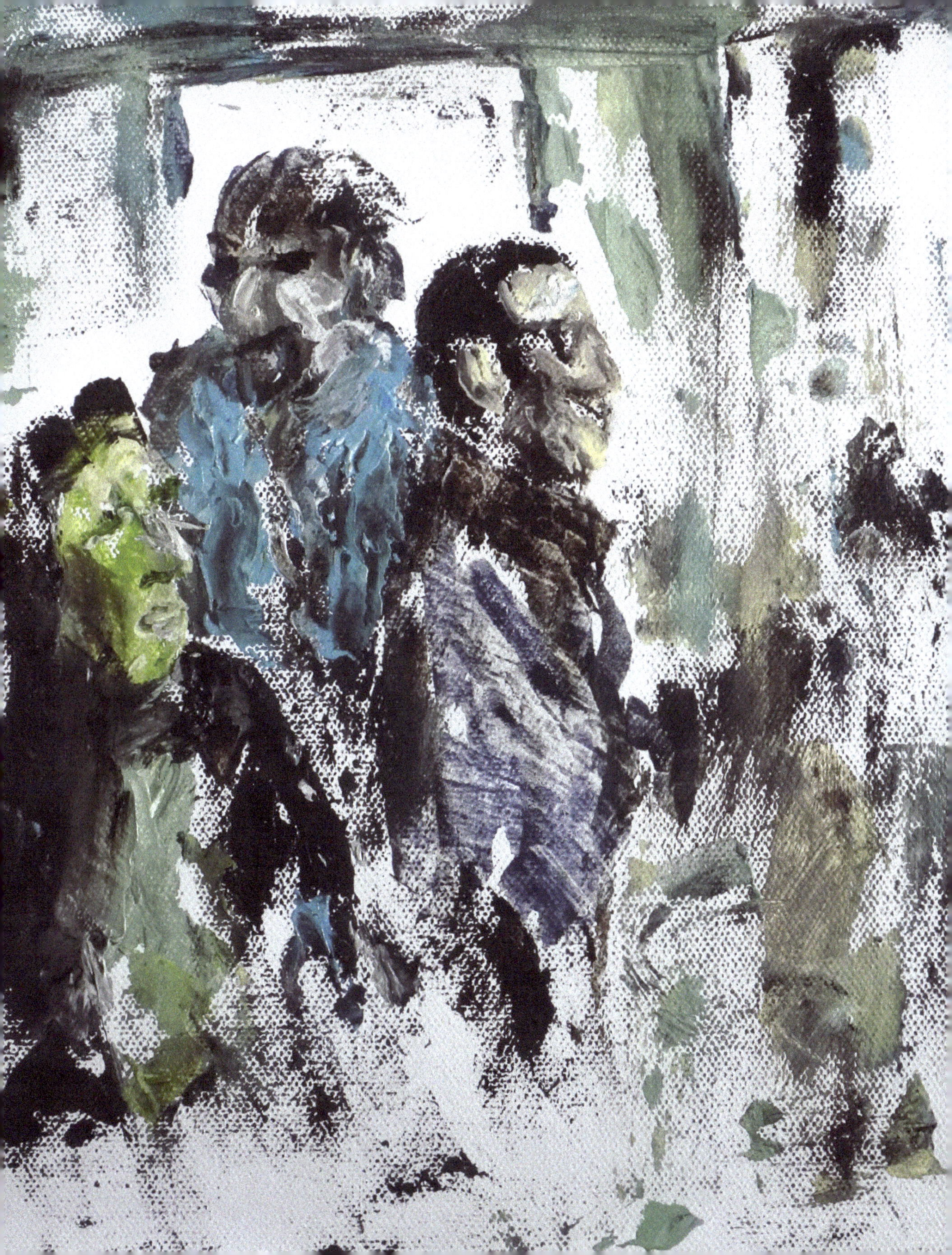

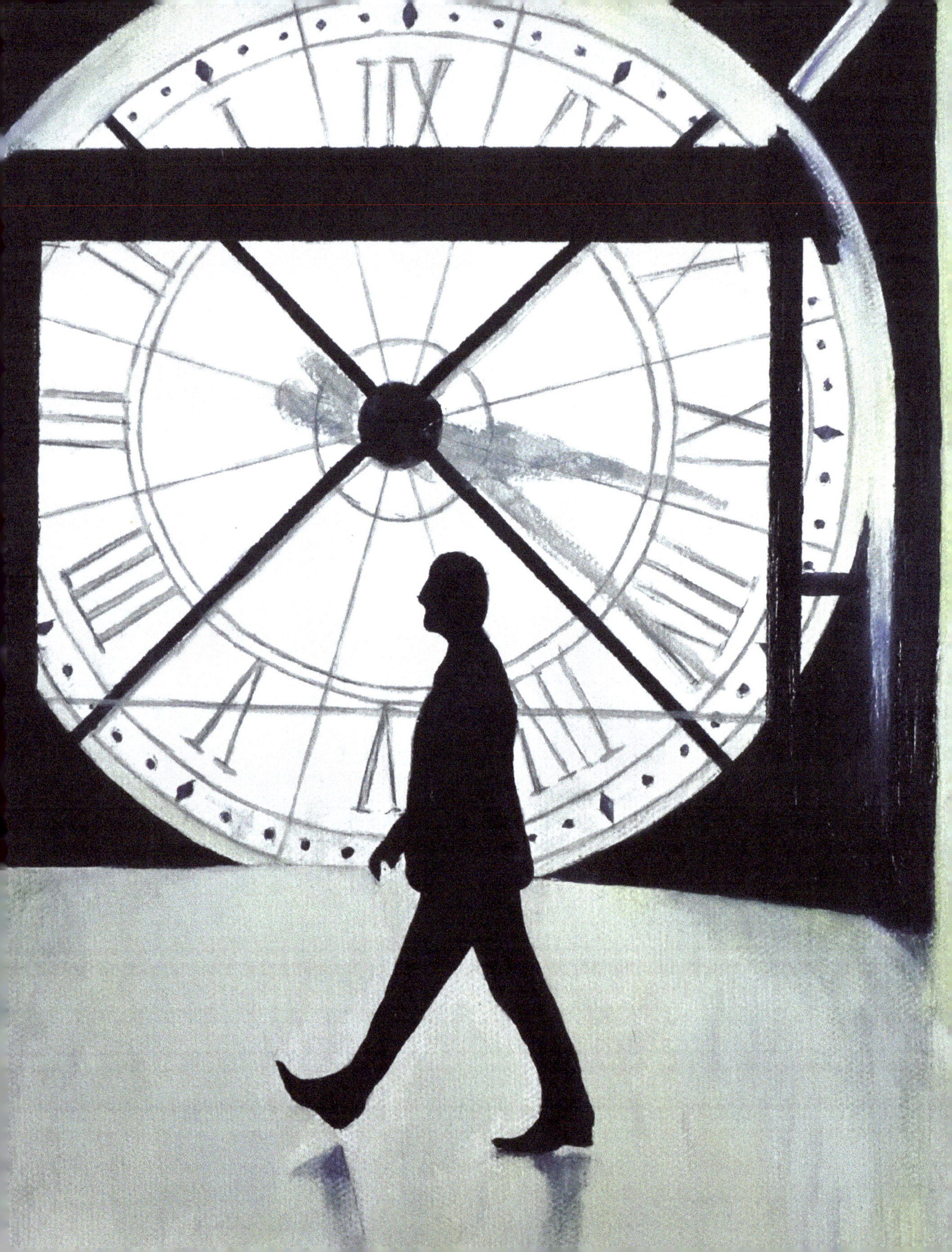

The Empire – The 'Official' Version

The Empire is not a monarchy. It isn't a republic. It's not a dictatorship either. And it's certainly not to be viewed as an oligarchy. It's a monopoly of sorts – good in mood and sentiment. (Hearts and minds.)

It is a regulated civilisation.

And at the top is the Emperor.

The Emperor thought it strange that sometimes time goes fast. And it seems to go faster the older you get.

At other times, everything can stretch out and time appears to be going in slow motion. And just when you think you have a hand on that, time throws a wobbly and goes in reverse.

Experts call it memory-time, but it isn't.

It isn't even retrospection.

It's mainly Hindsight.

Sometimes, time even stops.

Rotates. Repeats.

There's no point in asking what time it is. It's all perfectly normal here.

No one wears (or needs) watches.

It makes no sense, Welcome to the Empire.

From the average citizen's point of view, the Empire is a realisation of common good – a perfect societal model where inclusion is the archetypal exemplar.

Even though there are 'the rich', no one is poor.

Everyone's material needs are met in a timely and appropriate fashion, and the results of the most important rolling measure of collective satisfaction, 'the People's Pulse', is regularly taken and widely publicised (visualise spaceships skywriting on windless days).

The stock market doesn't exist, because the Empire owns everything. Buying and selling businesses is unnecessary and everyone is on the same side in the free market. (Which really is free.)

It isn't Utopia, it isn't Nirvana and it isn't Heaven either (you can make up your mind about the realities of those 'states').

Although it is not perfect, the Empire stands for a beneficial sense of being and a reality that's striving for continual improvements in quality, process and delivery. (Now, where have you heard that before?)

Whoever came up with the original idea must have been pretty clued-in.

Doing away with different tiers of government – in fact, getting rid of any traditional form of government – is definitely worth voting for. Elections are redundant. There is no opposition. Rule by consensus – where everybody is in agreement. It's the best way forward for everyone – no matter her or his station in life (Town Hall, Grand Central, Watercloset or St Pancreas, etc.).

In the Empire, generally speaking, everything is absolutely 'tickety-boo'!

No one is to be left behind, left out, disadvantaged, or misses the train.

The Empire – In Actuality

Self-contained as an area of existence, the Empire is indistinguishable from the universe you are familiar with and instantly recognisable for its day-to-day foibles, and unjust social structure forced on the poor unfortunates who misguidedly elected the lawmakers in the first place. Because it's compulsory to vote, 'Mr and Mrs Smith' have no choice. (What a ridiculous notion – in this day and age; no one would believe that to be true, even in a fairy story!) The Empire is well established in the alternate universe. It's not a paradise, it's more of a paradigm. As you may have gathered by now (unless you're slow on the uptake), it is a strange place.

There is a formal legislature in the Empire – but not one that anyone could acknowledge, because this 'Government' enacted such preposterous rules and ludicrous decrees it was structurally flawed from the ballot box upwards.

If there had been an Opposition, it would be far easier to recognise and theoretically legitimise – particularly as it would never be forced to put anything into practice (even though it may have been full of 'good' ideas). But the Constitution didn't allow for an Opposition, as complete accord was enshrined in the Charter of Rights and anything less than perfection and absolute agreement was banned. All was sweetness and light across the Empire. Parliamentary sessions were so quick you'd miss them, and it was impossible to find them on Cable TV. Nobody watched the free-to-air channels. Which, of course, is why they were free.

In the Empire, time doesn't work the way you are accustomed for it to work, nor do the universal laws of physics or motion. Time doesn't go from A to B – and can't be followed in a straight line – it is circular, though irregular, rather like the 389 bus route. The upshot is, if you wait long enough, you'll arrive at the point you left. Some call this the theory of relative transport. It's perfectly acceptable to get on or off at any juncture. You don't have to wait for a designated stop. You don't even have to wait. Many find it quite fun to re-join the journey before they embarked in the first place. It's not so much a case of 'déjà vu' as 'c'est quoi ce bordel' (or 'WTF' in English).

Time discrepancy is another reason you can never find anything worth watching on TV. Crap programming is another. Uninterested, unentertained and utterly unimpressed, the general population* goes about its business. It is only on closer inspection (and introspection) that the real truth, if there ever is such a thing, emerges.

*Note: On reflection, the term 'general population' is ridiculous, as it's either duplication/superfluous or a military state entirely made up of Generals.

Yellow sky at night is the Emperor's delight. Yellow sky in the morning is usually missed because most people are asleep. If they were awake they would undoubtedly wonder what the shepherd had to worry about.

Perhaps it was the misspelling of his lifelong calling that caused the most concern.

The missing vowel is an unspeakable occupational oversight. After all, who would like their profession spelt as Enginer, or even Ngineer, Prim Minister, Firman, Scintist, Tacher, Nurs or Ditor.

Or perhaps the sheep herder had other problems.

You heard it here first.

It may have been the cut price of chops, but more likely it was that wool was becoming yesterday's fashion fabric – producing shear terror in a man who not only called the land home, but, more importantly, lived off the sheep's back.

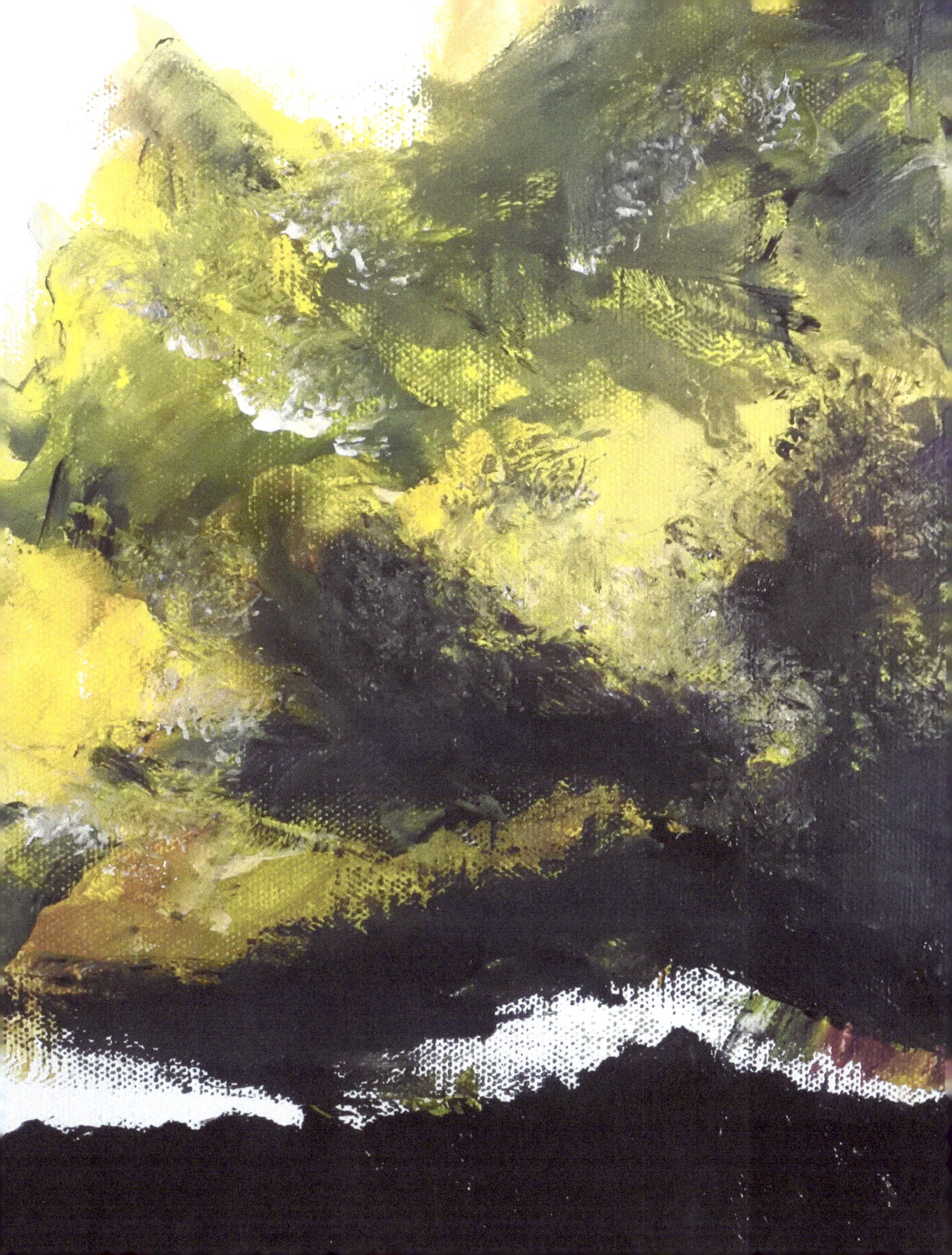

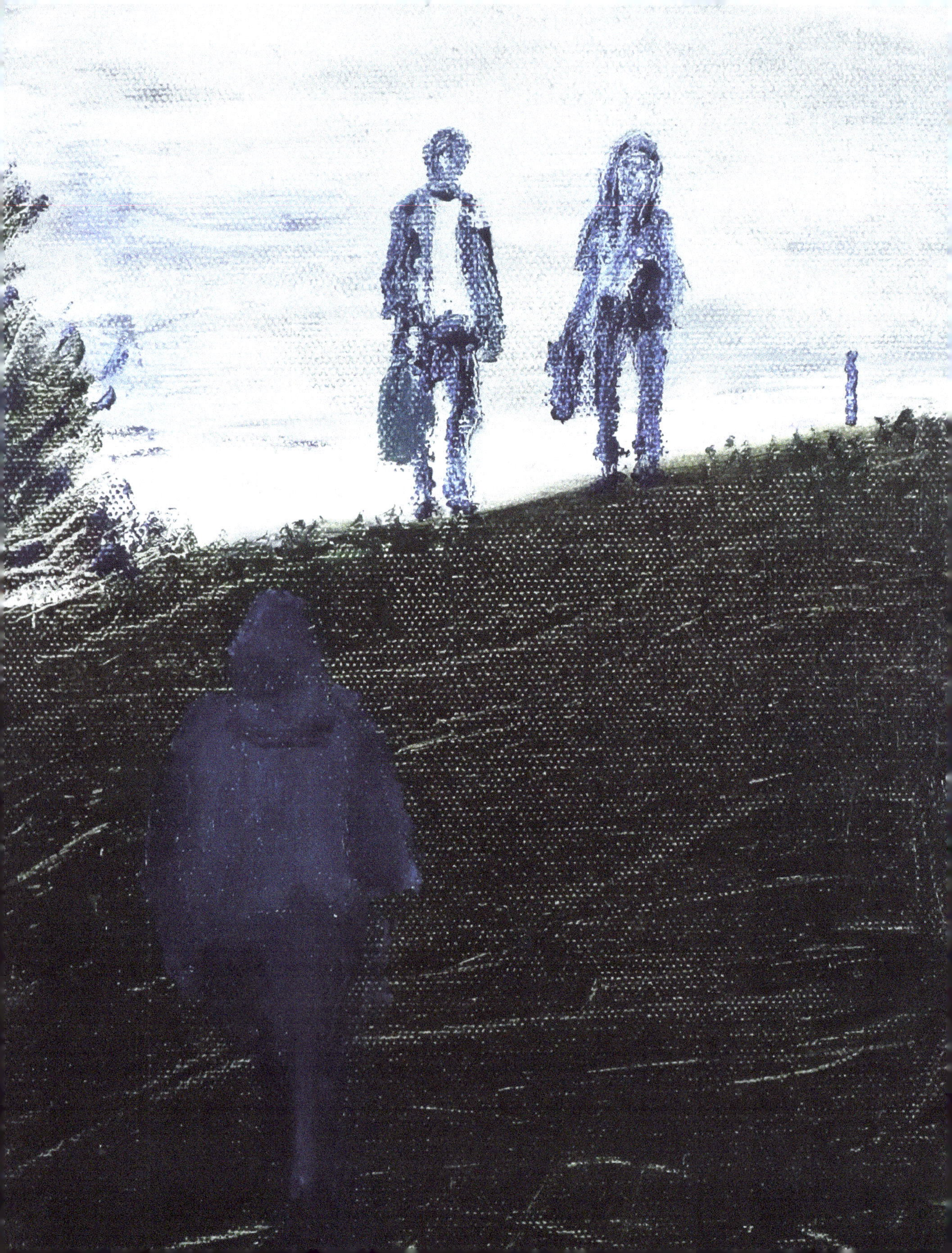

Out of the City

The Emperor usually lived in Anonymity.

Anonymity was the capital of the most important State in the Empire. But it wasn't conducive to the Emperor's need for quiet solitude.

The Emperor longed for a more simple life and plotted for many years how to achieve his goal on a permanent basis. A visit to the countryside was well overdue.

Every now and again, his mind raced back to early memories and more simple times. There's more food for thought when you don't have much on your plate, and across the Empire no one minds if you ask for second helpings. The request is appreciated, because it means you liked what was provided in the first place and it's also a nice compliment to their kitchen staff.

The Emperor always had a terrible sense of direction. It continually came as a surprise every time he ended up at a place he hadn't planned to visit. And being the Emperor, this happened quite often.

He found there was something comforting about walking at random in any direction in the countryside, and just before you think you might be lost, you intersect with a path created solely by repeated foot or animal traffic that leads you on to where you actually wanted to go in the first place.

The Emperor referred to these occurrences as 'relief paths'.

Others inaccurately call them 'track backs'.

On his way out of the 'big smoke' of Anonymity, the Emperor decided to visit some old acquaintances. He didn't have much to say, but had a need to be near familiar faces and unpaved, well-trodden places.

'Lucky for you, I'm far better equipped to be a communicator,' said Narrator. 'Not only do I know how to start a conversation, I'm very capable of keeping it going.'

The Emperor wouldn't actually show his face, but there were plenty of old tricks he used – to appear to be someone else. It was a type of identity borrowing – adopting a disguise, camouflaging his presence.

Another technique he'd observed was to simply act in the most natural and conspicuous manner possible and no one would notice you were up to anything underhand. If you were good enough you could go completely unnoticed. But it took a great deal of practice. Some call it hiding in plain sight.

The Emperor had years to rehearse – carefully managing his appearance to perpetuate inconspicuousness. This meant it was unlikely he'd ever be noticed, and even if he was observed, he banked on not being recognised. Most of those he called his 'close friends' didn't even know they knew him.

It was complicated, getting to know the Emperor.

'Xenophobia, like Algebra, is nothing of which to be scared!' said Fred (not his real name).

Fred was a grammatical pedant (in a manner of speaking), but when it came to Geometry, he was directionless.

He wasn't completely obtuse, but this subject simply didn't stack up for Fred – he needed another angle of attack.

All through school his teachers told him to think laterally, but Fred never got on a roll.

Years later, at odds with most of his associates (you are welcome to use an alternative noun or descriptor here – Fred always did), he summed it all up, as many had done before, and left the city drudge for a cleaner, more rounded way of life.

Basically, he and countless others decided to bale.

The Emperor was jealous.

Many of the country areas were just opening up after a series of what can only be described as catastrophes. It was testament to the hardy people who espoused a more natural way of life eschewing the buzz of the city – much preferring the sound of Apidae.

On his walks, the Emperor made a note that more should be done for these country folk, the salt of the earth. He surmised it seemed to be a case of 'out of sight, out of mind' for equitable Government support, and those who assembled in the biggest numbers and made the loudest noise were the ones that were more favourably funded.

Most of the local population were tethered, due to their good nature, to daily responsibilities to livestock or nurture for the land. Or they couldn't be bothered wasting their time, money and genial affability to travel again to the metropolis to outline their case to ears that would not listen.

For his trips, the Emperor packed lightly. He didn't use a suitcase, as he never found one with wheels that went in the direction he wanted to head. They also made it much more obvious that you were going on a trip somewhere than if you carried a holdall or a small backpack. He didn't use supermarket trolleys for the same reason.

Not long ago, before the weather turned, he visited nearby Wizard Lake on Crater Island just before the latest series of eruptions further devastated the area, temporarily ending the prosperity and employment that 'new environment' sightseeing had brought to the local population as an adjunct to their agricultural income (pittance).

Shortly after that low impact activity had to shut down, exciting new adventure holidays were developed for city dwellers to take up the slack. At the start of each exhilarating tour, participants were supplied with attractive 'fitted' coveralls, which were worn over the light shirts and walking shorts they all seemed to prefer – no matter how chilly the morning had started. The day's schedule involved taking part in a succession of ludicrous activities. First, abseiling onto the cinder cones for photo opportunities. Then, if the tourists survived that excitement, they were shown how to inflate their previously pocket-sized multiform (located in the outer top left chest compartment of their overalls) to canoe across the lake. The vessel then metamorphosed shortly after arrival on the far shoreline to catapult each enthralled guest high into the air (vertical take-off) before transforming into powered wing suits (orange hi-vis) in mid-air. Via this method, everyone was flown back in full goose formation behind the team leader (if they were still alive, or via auto sat navigation if not) to the mainland, where the events concluded with a mug of organic vegetable soup on the beach and a diminished group photo.

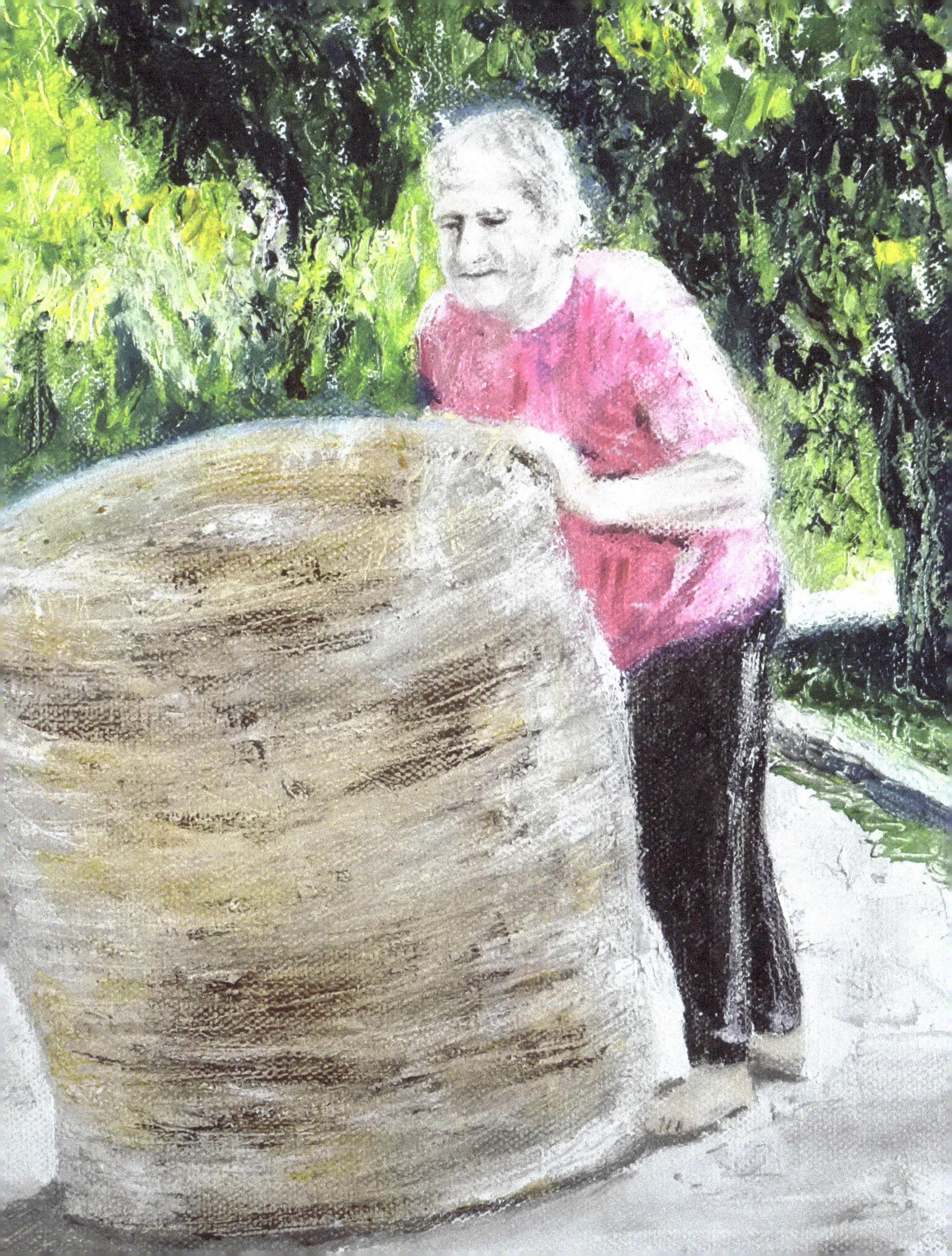

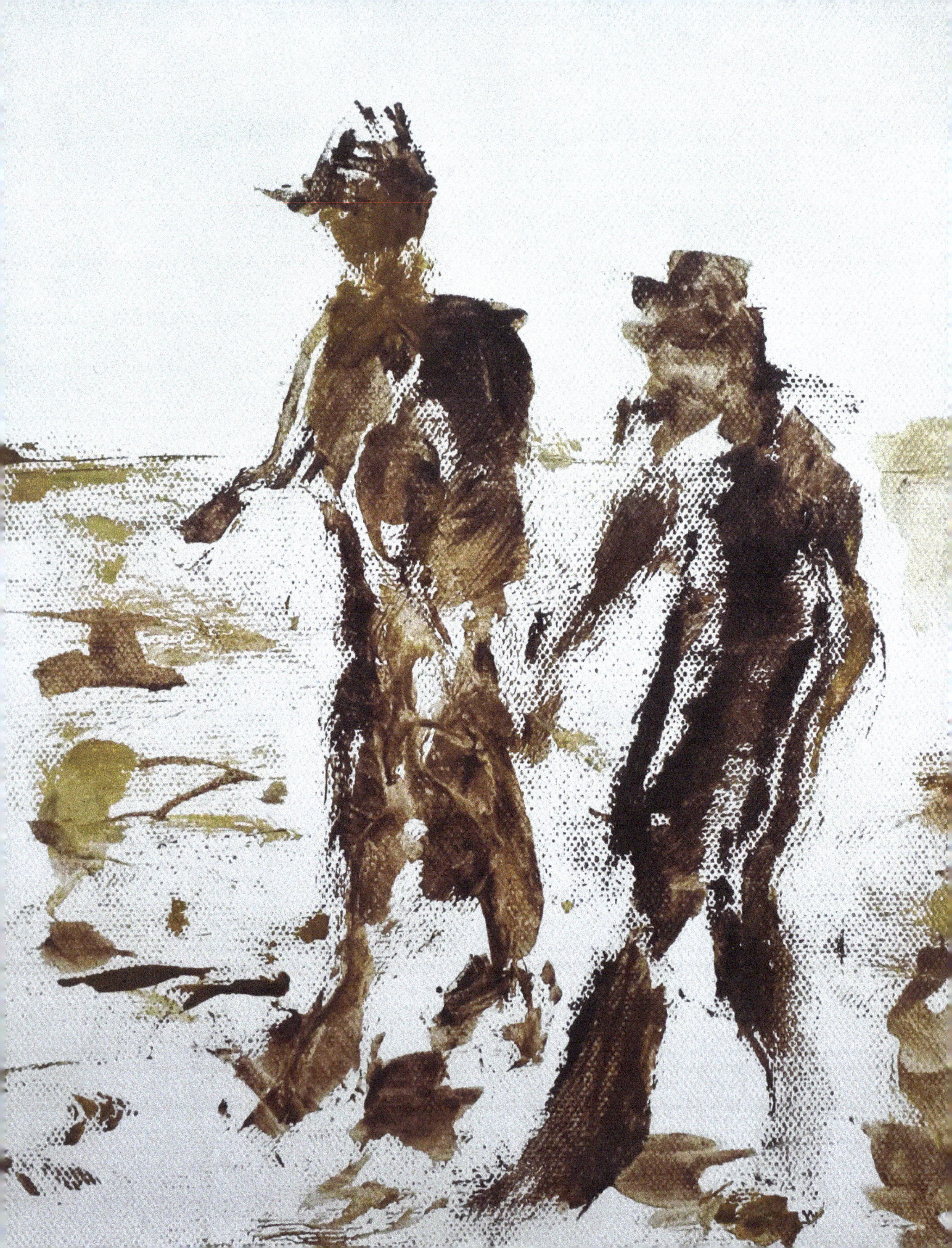

Carrying his theodolite, Caldera Ringmaster made slow progress measuring the new terrain with his greenest assistant.

'For goodness sake, look where you're going.' (Caldera didn't actually say 'goodness'.)

He was beginning to question the younger man's common sense.

Alex the apprentice was wearing his new T-shirt featuring a Hop-Hip Artist, misprinted so it appeared halfway between his stomach and his chest.

He thought he looked pretty cool.

Caldera didn't think much of Alex's fashion sense either.

Like the underground magma, Caldera was hot under the collar. The last thing he needed was another eruption – it may be good for the travel company's upcoming marketing, but he couldn't bear to be a respondent in another event evaluation survey.

It came as a shock when the tourism industry's initial enthusiasm died down. Tour operators found it difficult to recruit replacements as the previously reliable supply of instructors started to dwindle, then expire.

Never the type to miss an opportunity, an enterprising video media and website company developed an extensive eight-minute induction, training and safety manual to be delivered online to fill the gap. But this 'self-help guide' failed to hit the confidence-building sweet spot. Either the 'target' audience for these types of 'adventure' activities was not as stupid as the sales development team assumed, or there weren't as many idiots (with a death wish) that were estimated in pre-sales meetings and brainstorming sessions.

As time elapsed, it became increasingly difficult to sell any type of adventure 'holidays', so advertisement headlines and subsequent body copy messaging resorted to 'almost giveaway pricing' with 'premium packages featuring short stays and one-way travel'. Ultimately, 'free funeral insurance' was trialled with little take-up. Were anyone to actually read the fine print they would have realised they couldn't have claimed on the policy anyway. The final nail in the venture's coffin was applied when the local Regional Tourism Co-operative unanimously appointed an international award-winning creative advertising agency to the overall account – after an extensive five-minute credentials pitch by a mate of a mate over a beer at the bowling club on a Friday morning – in a completely open and transparent process with all selection criteria publicised widely in announcements with a closing date for submissions that occurred yesterday.

In a carefully managed and intricately researched multi-platform marketing initiative funded by local businesses and tour operators, the new ad agency spent heavily on conceptualising, writing, designing, storyboarding, and (in an Empire-first) filming in 4D, editing, audience previewing, rewriting, refilming, re-editing and repreviewing. In research, the campaign received the highest-ever consumer approval rating. Unfortunately, there was no budget left to purchase any mass media airtime or space in newspapers and magazines (these last two had to all intents and purposes ceased to exist anyway). So not one member of the general public, potential short-break or longer holidaymaker targets ever saw the finished advertisements.

The correct industry term is that the campaign fizzed. The good news is that it didn't damage the creative agency's reputation in the slightest – and the advertisements were used in their self-promotional activity to attract new clients – boasting of their effectiveness in achieving the highest-ever consumer approval rating. On the back of this major success, the firm was predictably voted the Empire's #1 Tourism Advertising Agency for the third straight year.

The Art World Is Rapidly Descending

'Let's discuss visual art,' said Narrator.

'I'm no good at conversation,' the Emperor replied, before continuing, 'but I know what I like.'

'How do you know?'

The Emperor sighed. 'Just do. Never needed to think about it and have always appreciated aesthetics – from an early age. Probably before I was even created! If I didn't have to be the Emperor, I'd be a painter.'

Here are the IGN Brothers – Alexander, Benjamin and Desmond, informally (and better known) as AL, Ben and Des.

They're nominatively determined, outstanding citizens and great contributors to the Empire.

AL IGN is the Empire surveyor, Ben IGN the Empire peacemaker and Des IGN is a graphic artist.

The first worked closely with Caldera Ringmaster on Crater Island before it all became too hard (because of the softness of the ground).

Ben IGN soothed the locals' agitated condition, attempting (not 'at' but 'with' all costs) to avoid the legal action instigated against the Regional Tourism Co-operative for waste of money and amateurism.

Des designed the holiday brochures.

'Can't you be both?' asked Narrator (knowing what the answer would be).

'Can't be both. One's a vocation. The other is a responsibility.'

'I like that,' replied Narrator. 'When did you start to realise that being the Emperor doesn't require any natural ability?'

The Emperor disclosed, 'Take it from someone who knows...leadership is a role rather than a skill. It can be practised by anyone.'

'Trouble is,' Narrator reiterated, 'you are not just "anyone".'

A wise and famous artist once told the Emperor that painting is one-third the subject. One-third is the artist. But by far the biggest third is the art itself. The Emperor liked that.

Art can't be a democracy. It doesn't compute because it's not supposed to. That's why the Emperor both loves art and realises it drives him to distraction too.

It is one and the same, both different. It all adds up and when you add it up it doesn't. Can't live without it though.

At least on this last point, they both agreed.

'Who is your favourite artist?' asked Narrator.

'What a ridiculous question!' the Emperor roared. 'That's like asking me which is my favourite sunset. It's also like enquiring if I prefer women artists to men artists. I like artists.'

To the Emperor, sex made no difference. He knew it was pointless to exclude one section or specific group and to consider what are utterly extraneous factors, rather than simply focusing on the work itself.

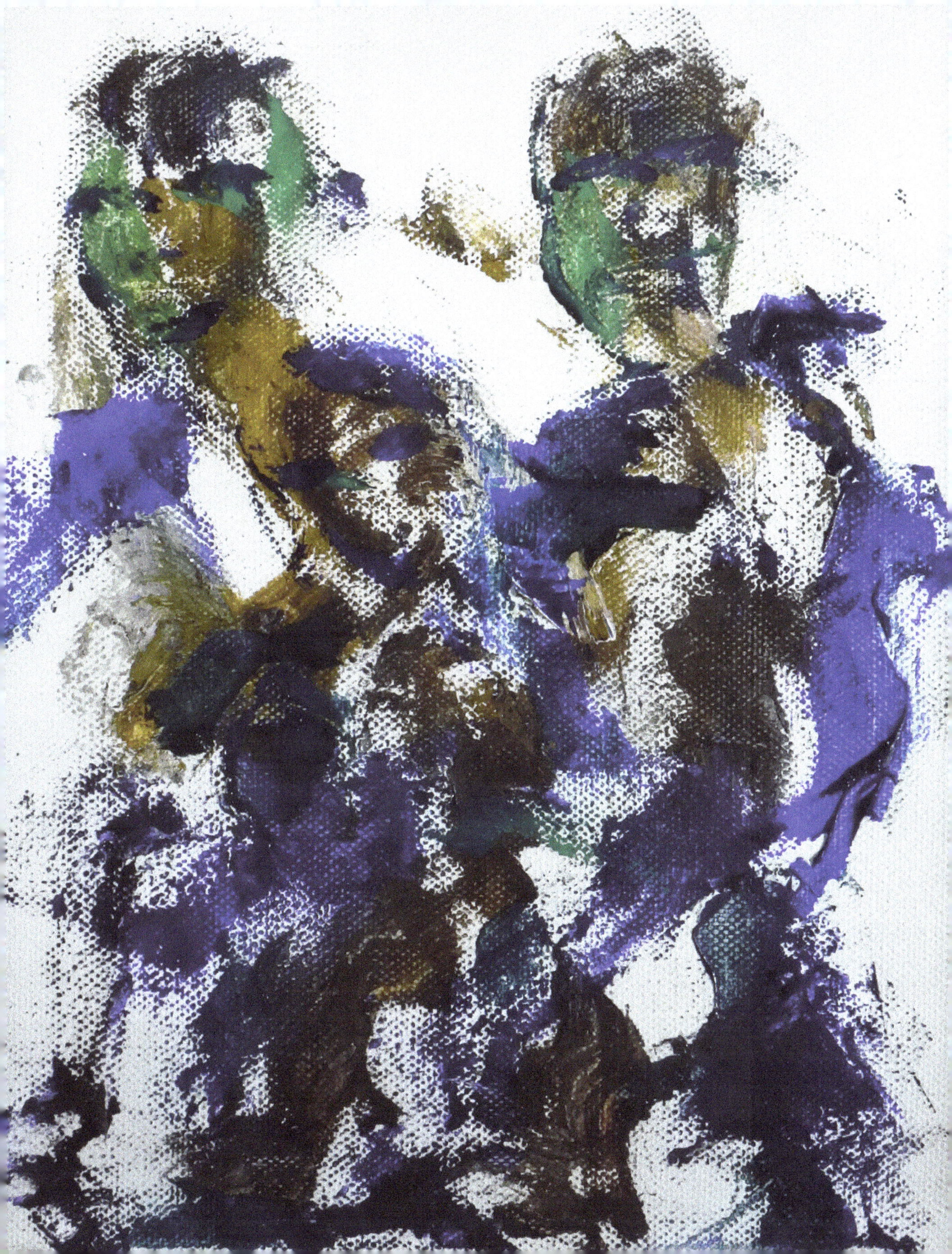

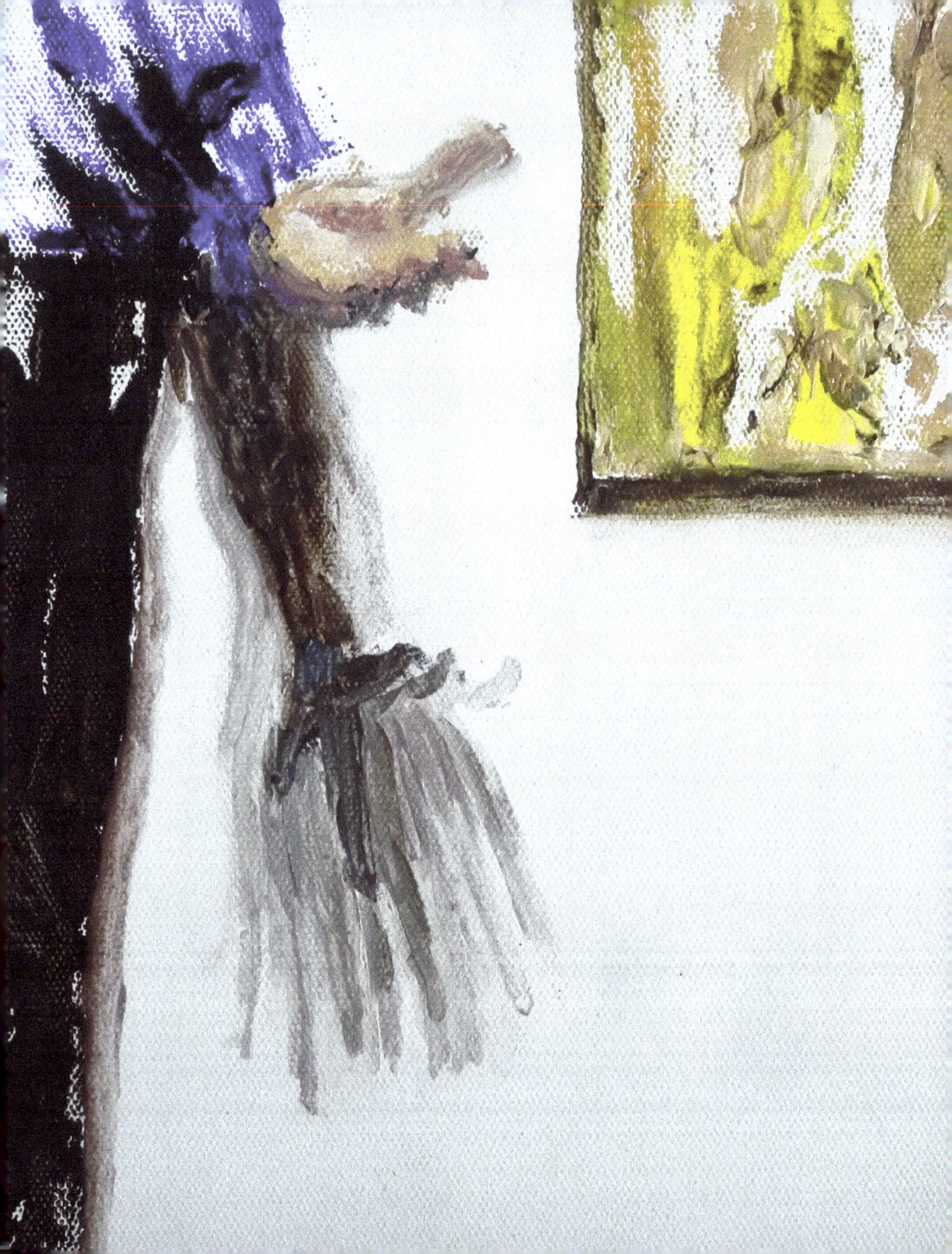

The Emperor liked this image and found its meaning to be purposefully ambiguous.

Should we focus on the gesticulation as if a curator is presenting the work, their hand lit by many light sources casting multiple readings? Or should we recognise the meaning of the outstretched hand as an artist pleading for just recompense?

It's a first Empire issue – cash in hand, or, more precisely, lack of cash in hand.

Even though the Treasury credited his account on the seventh of each month, the Emperor had never joined the Empire Bank, so had no way of withdrawing funds.

All in all, the Empire's banking system was in danger of falling to bits (which is not a reference to cryptocurrency).

Narrator mentions that when you take the letter 'i' out of 'debit', you innately lose the 'b' too.

Continuing this thread, the Emperor added that ideas-driven art had always driven him to distraction – going over his head completely.

Social politics, and the gambit of conceptual ideas – I leave any socio-political beliefs out of my appreciation of art, completely. I have enough political shit in my day-to-day existence. I find it intellectual claptrap. I'm not a curator or a critic or an arts administrator. They have their roles and their axe to grind, their row to hoe.

But what happened to the enjoyment of pure aesthetics – the idea of hanging something on the wall in your palace just because you like to walk past it regularly and appreciate it every time you do?

Oh, I didn't realise he could be so naïve, thought Narrator, fibbing to himself and sharing the thought with whoever was present.

Is it ignorance, whitewashing or, for that matter, blackwashing that's trying to compensate or, worse still, over-compensate for various injustices of the past? Without the right attitude and a policy of real inclusion, there's an absolute danger of repeating past errors, and that's more of a behavioural indictment, because today we should be standing in a position of enlightenment and knowledge.

Next thing, this sanctimonious rear end will accuse me of being a white Anglo-Saxon male, thought the Emperor. Even though I'm fairly sure I'm not, it wouldn't be my fault – in the slightest – if I were. Surely Narrator can't blame me for being created as I am, when I had no responsibility for my birth. He can't accuse me of having accountability for inequalities and wrongs of the past – in which I had no hand. Surely?

Narrator was professional at reading thoughts. It went with his job description, and his published stinging judgements were usually bang on.

'I know what you're thinking,' said Narrator. 'And yes, I bloody well can blame you. What makes you so immune from gender issues and social injustices – past and present?'

'My job title perhaps? the Emperor huffed.

The Emperor knew he was on controversial ground and dicey philosophical territory. Normally, he would purposely aggravate the issue by suggesting the introduction of male-only art prizes or art awards for the over-55s or prizes for the non-Indigenous population (just to be inclusive and equalise opportunities).

It wasn't just the art world that was descending on practitioners from great heights.

The Empire was going to hell in a hand basket – or, in today's terms, an illogically overstuffed (with toilet paper) shopping trolley.

With galleries and stages closing through public apathy and lack of funding, consumption was transferred rapidly (with appropriate appreciation diminution), from actuality on walls, plinths, performance or public spaces, and replaced by 'lazy likes' on hand-held communications devices, or, even worse, tiny screened watches (now, there's a misnomer).

The Emperor considered the arts world was becoming a good analogy for the parlous state of the Empire.

'So, Narrator, are you a fan of art?' The Emperor asked, attempting to turn the tables. He liked asking open questions, as the way in which the question was interpreted often revealed more than the answer itself.

'I'm no judge, but then again, when I see what's chosen for support, particularly in Empire-funded exhibitions, neither are the judges,' Narrator continued. 'Like most people, I suppose, I know when I see something I like. I used to go to galleries more often than I do now, which can be taken as my judgement on the current situation, the stuff they stick on walls. It's become too bloody elitist for me. Either that or they're biased in their views and favour the chosen few.

'Perhaps I'm old fashioned and art is a young-person's game. But I have to wonder how much of the stuff that's shown now will have any longevity. You know, "fashionable art" to me is like choosing a wedding dress that was in fashion at the time and when you look back at those images, all you can do is smile – or, worse still, laugh – and thank goodness today's brides don't look like that now.'

The Emperor tried not to show his disdain.

'Before I became professional,' Narrator confided, 'when I was growing up, I went to school with a mate and we hung around quite a bit from our early teens. We even played in a band together. We weren't successful, but we made a lot of noise. I don't think either of us – or any of us, apart from the lead guitarist – ever had a girlfriend, let alone a "groupie". And this guitarist guy only did because he was "good looking", or at least that's what he told us, and those who listened in every beat to the bar.

'I think it demonstrates how badly equipped we were as a band.

'Anyway, my friend went to art school but got booted out. He probably should have kicked on from there – it was quite a thing to be expelled from tertiary art in those days. He could have made a name for himself and launched his career on the back of it. All he needed to do was produce stuff, but he didn't even do that. I think that's why he was told to leave.

'Well, we lost touch, but years later I ran in to him again. He told me he was a carpenter and fitted kitchens. When I asked him what he did in his spare time, he told me he was going to evening classes in creative writing. I was stunned, because even though his great uncle was a famous philosopher and authors ran through his family, he didn't seem remotely interested in the written word. It all became clear when he told me it was a great way to meet the opposite sex.'

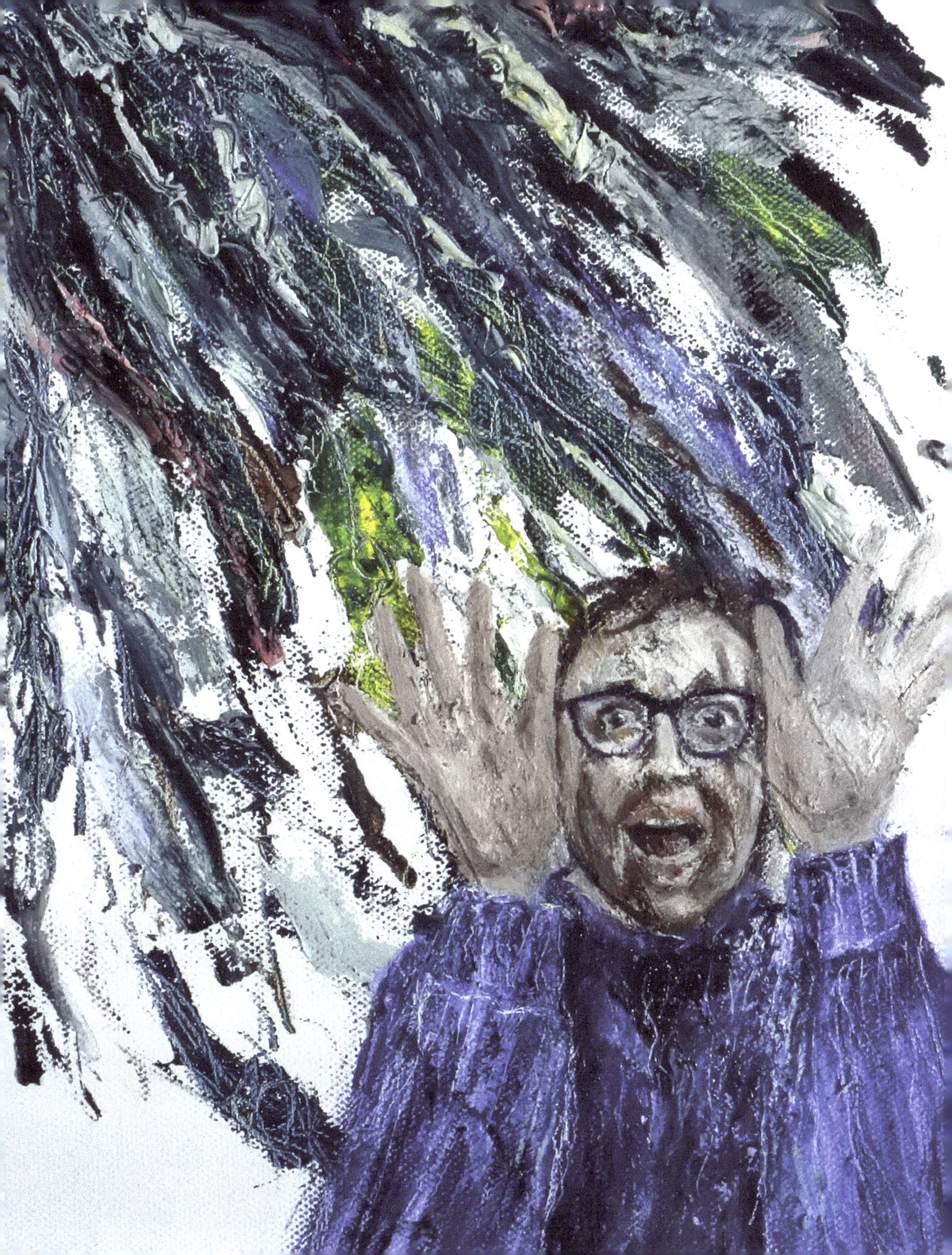

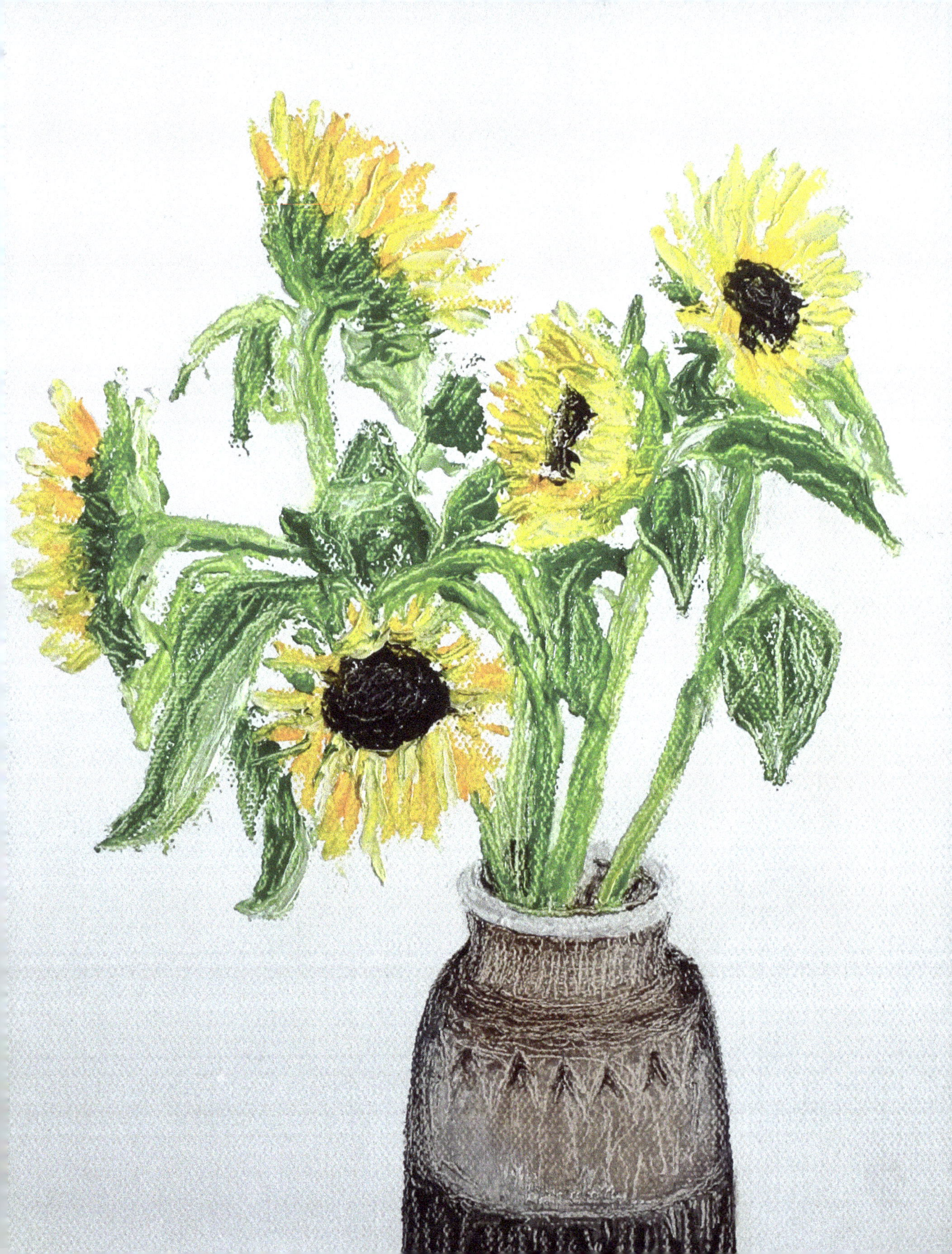

Funny things are Sunflowers, thought Antagonist. *I half expected Van Gogh to be right up at the top when I searched online, together with the Empire record pricing for art.*

Unfortunately, I was mistaken.

Instead, Sunflowers' symbolic meaning of unwavering faith and unconditional love was presented.

I consider much of human behaviour to be totally bizarre.

For example, whoever first came up with the idea to give cut flowers to a lover or as a gesture for family or friends must have been truly weird.

Here you go. I removed these naturally growing plants from their lovely environment so you could watch them slowly die in your own home.

Humans are unbelievable.

'So are you,' replied Retort. 'But it proves there is always more than one way to see things.'

So much for the arts, the Emperor thought.

No wonder it isn't better funded.

The Emperor liked adding fuel where it wasn't required… then sitting back and watching the results. He enjoyed stirring the intellectual pot.

Controversy was inherent to this role – although the Department of Extremely Civil Services wished the Emperor would keep his views to himself and consistently remain above and beyond commenting on 'problematic' issues.

The Emperor, though preferring to seem mute, considered it a duty to let everyone know where he stood. He was admired for putting the Empire and its citizens first and foremost.

The Emperor stood for diversity, accessibility and inclusion.

The only thing he didn't want included was himself.

For a long time now he thought the best way forward was to write himself out of the story – or ask the Author to – but at this stage there was no way he could walk away.

Apart from the fact that he had no natural successor, there was simply too much at stake – the whole Empire could collapse.

So what if it did? he thought.

Although he was normally considered to be in the best position to see, appreciate and deal with every scenario, the Emperor felt enormous disquiet.

What was it that consistently made him so remote – an outsider in his Empire?

Truth be told, it was becoming apparent it might not be 'his' Empire after all.

The old saying 'Give me a child until he is seven and I will show you the man' is fraught with danger in this day and age, thought the Emperor.

The prospect of giving anyone's child away to somebody else for seven years – least of all the clergy – is appalling. (Hopefully, it always was, is and will be.)

I'm sure it's impossible to predict with any certainty how people will grow up and what they will be like throughout their adult years. People change. They aren't black and white. Life isn't simple. It is like truth. It's not just one thing; there are unlimited shades of grey.

Take me, for instance.

My position is not negotiable. My birthright is that I become Emperor. I was born to this position and I am supposed to uphold the traditions of leadership. It is expected of me. And for quite a while – certainly many more than seven years – I believed that's how it should be. It was my destiny. That's how I used to be.

I don't feel that way now. For example, I was viewed as a city dweller – seen as sophisticated, culturally connected, 'in the know' and leader of the 'set'. Now I'm more of a country bumpkin and I like it this way. I value the innumerable nuances that only country time and country space provide. I've had enough of the big smoke.

Don't get me wrong. I know it's not for everyone. Truisms get their name because they are based on truth. But for me the 'ism' is the giveaway. If the maxim had been 'Give me the Emperor until he is seven and I'll show you the adult Emperor', I would respond that's false. I'm the proof and that's my truth.

'Jeez, you're full of yourself,' exclaimed Antagonist. 'Do you think anyone cares?'

'Quite clearly, apart from the title, I'm like anyone else. That's how I'm cut out to be. My titular role is the problem. It sets me apart.'

'What? Like looking into the sun. My word, you're full of it.'

'Exactly. You're not supposed to, because it would stop you from seeing anything ever again.'

With that, the Emperor withdrew.

It was getting late and the sun was beginning to set.

The story goes that when the Emperor was young he followed in the equine traditions of the position. It was his right to rein though he decided early on he had no desire to accompany anyone down the bridal path.

Not a natural, he was so determined to stay in the saddle, his riding style was completely non-existent.

Frankly, it was embarrassing.

He looked like he was 'glued on' horseback.

Luckily, no images (either still or moving) have survived.

Steed, his favourite horse, had no desire to get out of second gear, thus he never went much above walking pace, which suited them both just fine.

In return for riding lessons, the Emperor had to 'muck out' the stables, which left him with a lifelong resolve to never put up with shit in adulthood.

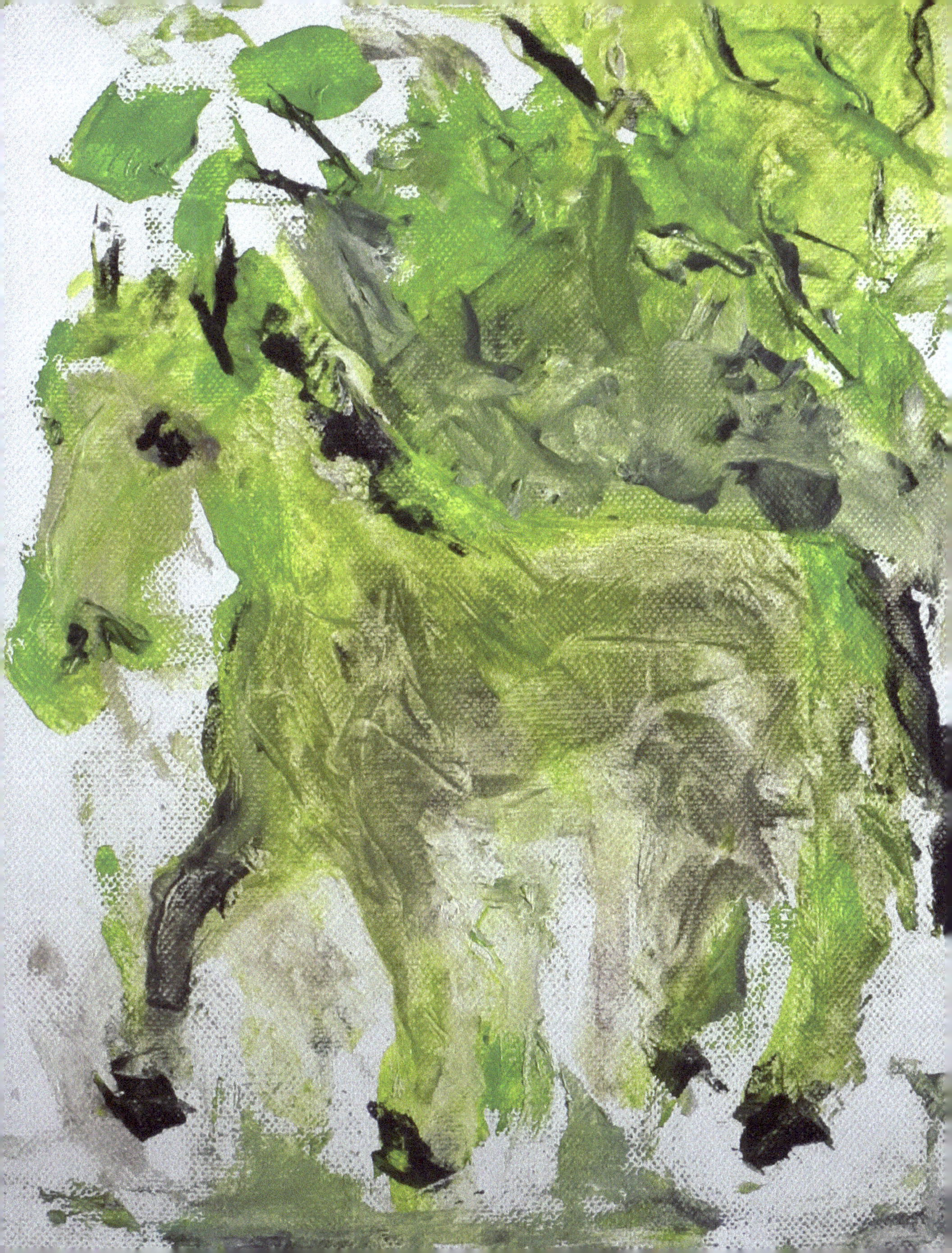

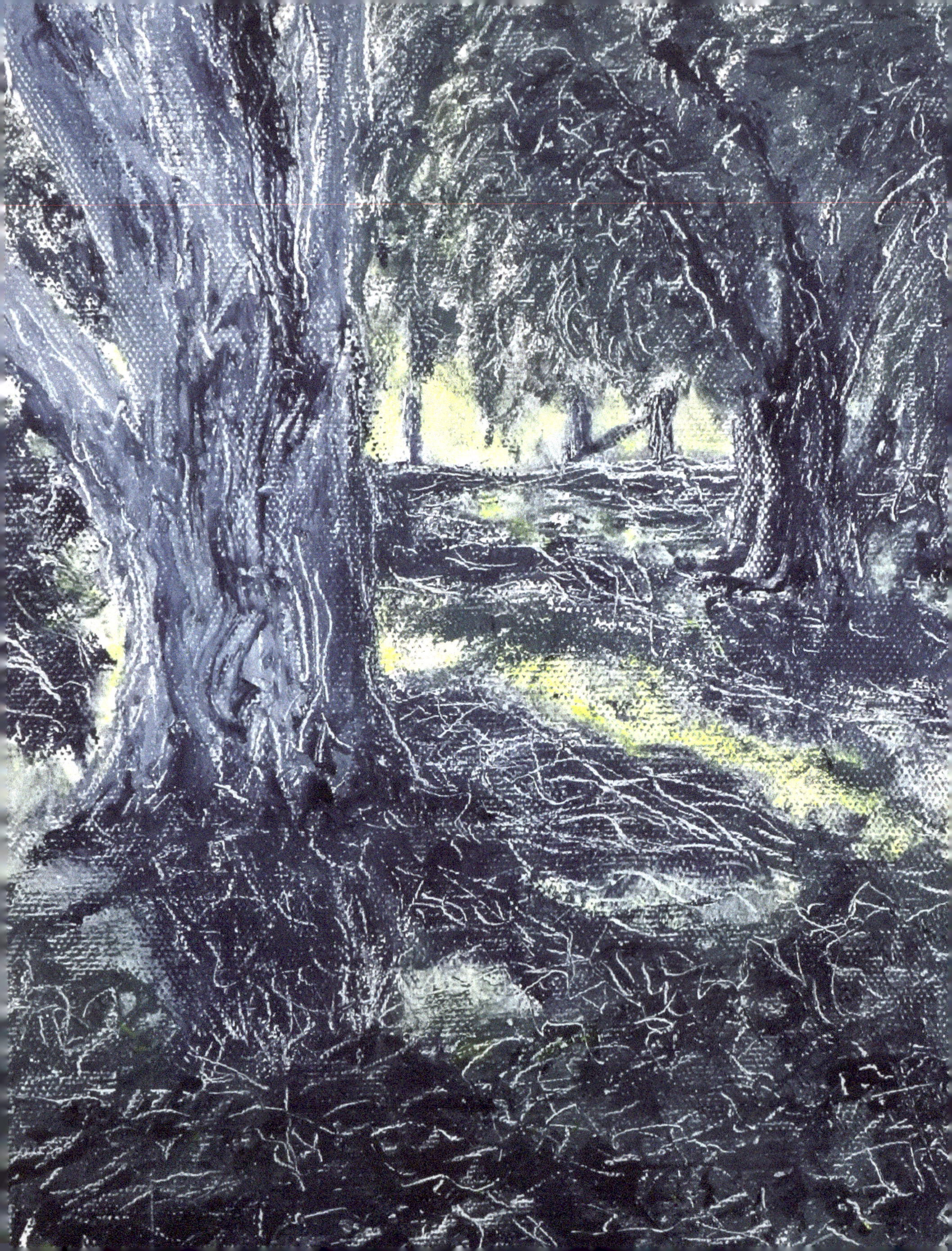

The Emperor loved the play of light through foliage. In a gentle breeze he imagined the landscape becoming animated and alive – the sight always lifted his spirits.

With his thoughts, he was never alone. Trouble was, he couldn't escape them either. So he imagined taking long walks, mostly closing his eyes as he found it easier to visualise the details.

He also debated non-stop and at length with his silent, cerebral confidants.

Querulous is a strange word one thought declared, followed by...but there's no use complaining about it. There aren't enough day-to-day simple pleasures another thought thought. No one argued.

The Emperor took his amusements when and where he could. He smiled to himself (and his metaphysical friends) and moved forward.

The next day brought a new dawn. The overall mood was changing for the better. It may have been the country air or the desire for enlightenment.

Timeless has a different meaning in the alternate universe. (Not to be confused with timelessness – which is an ageless, rarely seen, possibly mythical water creature that lives a solitary existence in Outtawedloch.)

However, whilst we are on the subject, or should that be whilst we were on the subject, or at other times, whilst we will be on the subject, the similarity between the alternate universe and alternate reality is/was/will be becoming clearer.

They both have/had/will have the same difference.

This is making me tense... and them very similar, except when the parallel universe pops its head up (which it never does) – well, it does but you never see it because it runs parallel and stays just out of sight over the horizon.

And by the way, there is no such thing as the Flat Empire Society.

Quite why no one has yet come up with a better definition for a pun than 'it is something that plays a pun the meaning of a word' further condemns the state of the Empire.

It's not so much perverse as multiverse, although it's somewhat converse too.

And this does not refer to a brand of footwear available across the Empire, as someone had already registered the name – for a brand of surreptitious recording devices. It was considered relevant. The fact that the devices could be located in the soles of ordinary sneakers, made no difference. Coincidentally, they doubled as telephones too.

Now we've cleared that up, it's back to the Empire. You know, the one that sort of looks like yours and you identify with. Except never end a sentence with a preposition – or you'll end up in a completely syntactically unsound, confused obfuscation.

Funny how taut and tautology mean different things.

Now you have a greater understanding of why the Emperor wanted out.

Getting on with the Emperor was a major problem for the Court's Jester, whom his close contacts referred to as 'CJ'. He'd been present for as long as anyone could remember – it seemed like forever – then some. Everyone assumed he'd originally been brought on to entertain the young Emperor and jolly him along, make japes, invent ruses to keep him entertained (that sort of thing), or at the very least keep him occupied.

That wasn't the truth at all.

Banners nicknamed the Court's Jester 'the OWL' and it wasn't just in jest.

Regularly, he played the role, but everyone knew he was nobody's fool.

A unique actor with a highly complex list of characters, he suffered from multiple personalities and was as scary as a clown can be.

His performance look said one thing but his act was something else.

The promotional poster showed his psychic sidekick, who resembled a big, white rubber duck. She was okay, because all agreed she fitted the bill.

And in the background, his support team of operatives moved silently and usually unobserved.

In these days of apparent crisis and unease, being the Jester was a serious business.

His actual duties were very different from those in the job advertisement he'd answered. Having sent in his CV and a video of himself performing stand-up, and clips he'd borrowed from social media posts (actually stolen without attribution) that had been captured on various phones while he verbally assaulted passers-by on street corners, he was appointed without ever having met the selection committee or auditioned for the role.

He wondered why.

When he found out what his actual job entailed, he considered taking the Court's Human Resource Department to the Industrial Relations Hoo-Ha, but he decided against it as:

1) He wasn't 100% sure he qualified as human
2) There were no other positions he was suitably qualified to fill
3) Alternative career openings for a Court's Jester were few and far between, and
4) He was having an absolute hoot in the job.

So, shortly after being appointed, he found he'd become the Court's spokesperson – effectively the Empire PR man – and his day-to-day role became increasingly preoccupied with 'issues management'.

Where issues didn't exist beforehand, he had an uncanny ability to create them.

A bit like adding fire to the fire, he was quite incendiary.

It regularly became a laughable situation – not 'funny haha'.

Thing was, absolutely everyone in the Empire had their own issues and it would all have been seen as nonsense if the problems weren't so widespread and so serious. General unease and discontent was rising.

The Empire was in trouble.

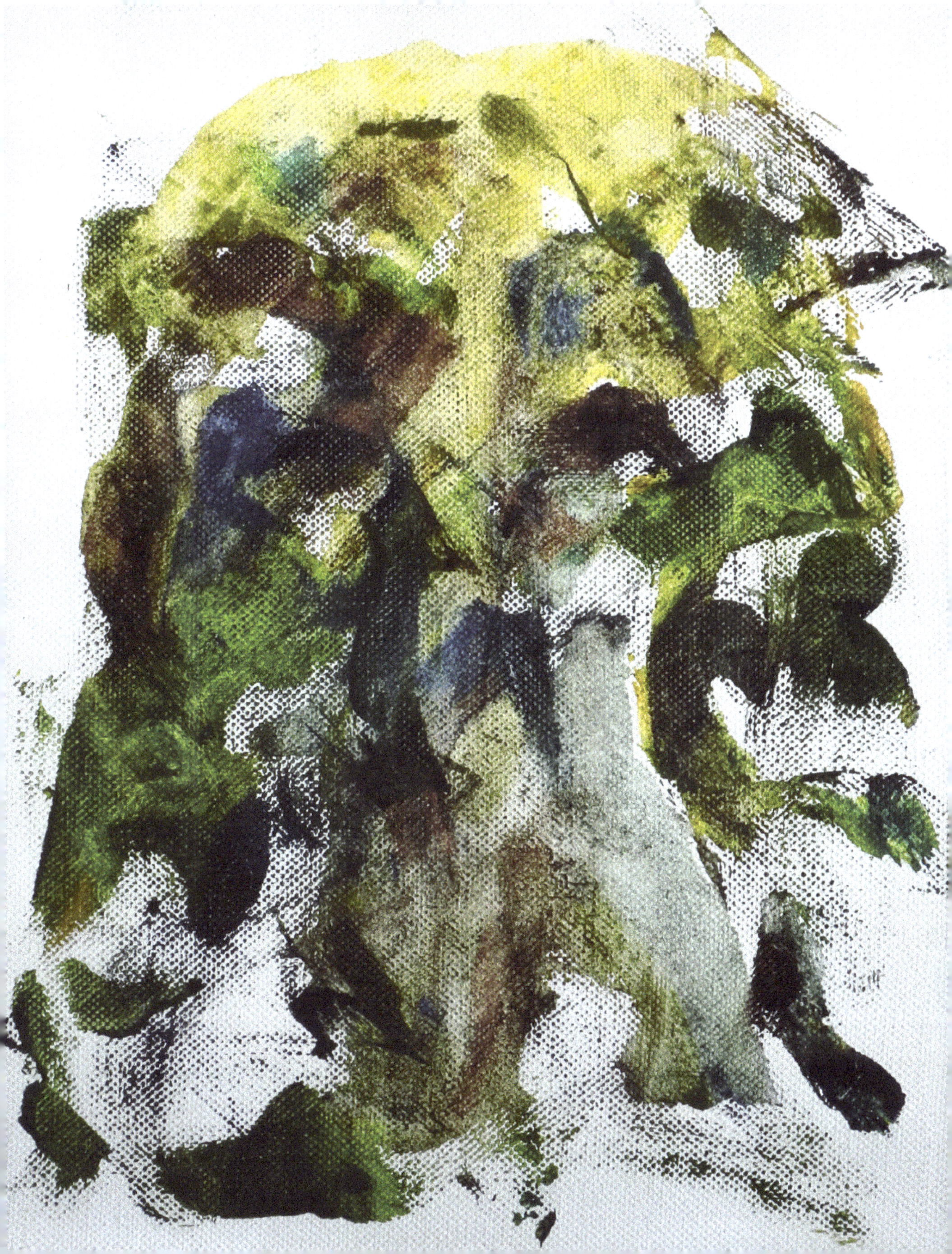

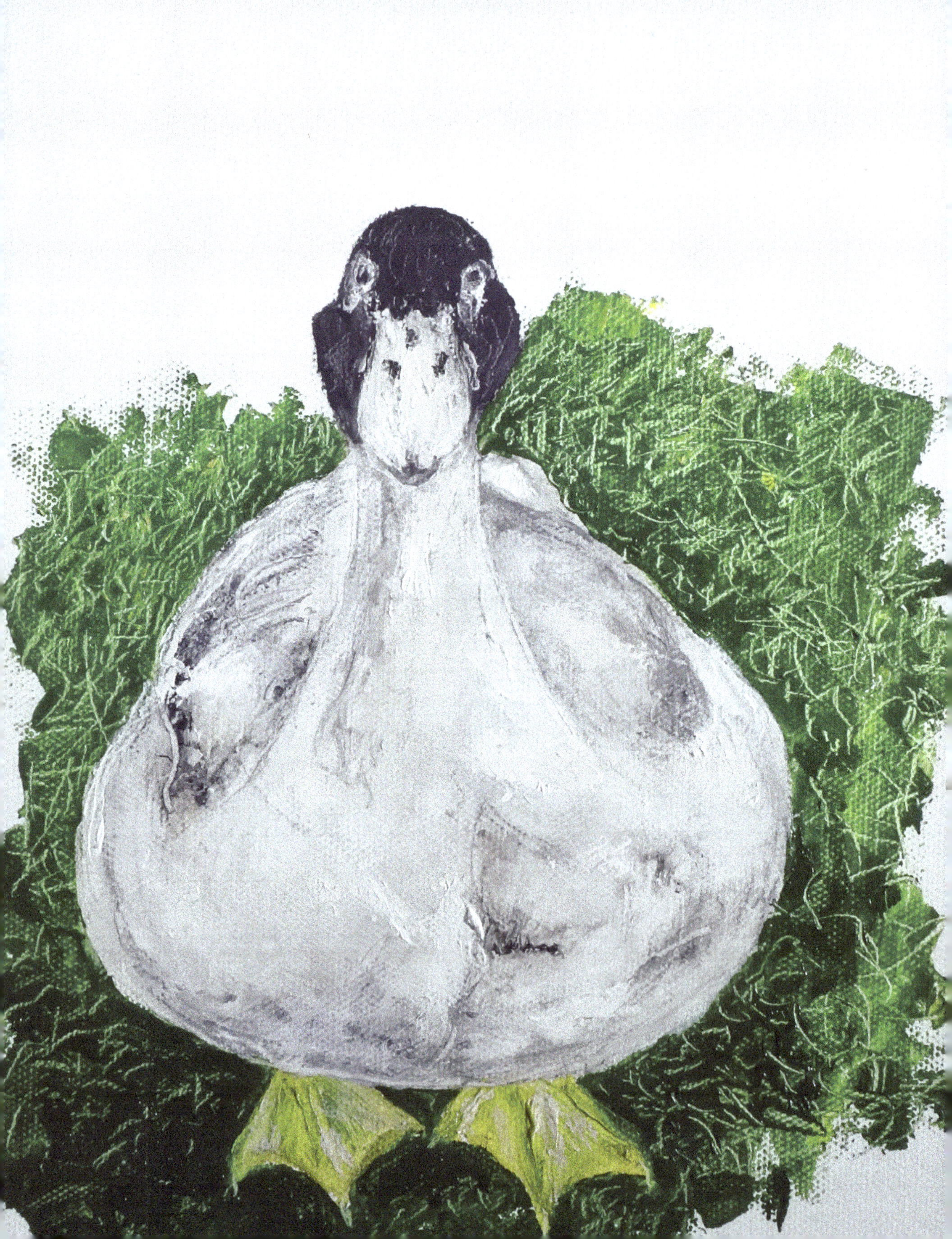

Dany became known as 'Thumb Duck', a widely celebrated abstract artist.

Originally a traditional painter, she created finely crafted and exquisitely rendered portraits and landscapes, holding the brush dexterously in her mouth.

Unfortunately, using this method, her career did not take off.

Changing tack, she now stands in paint and waddles her way across the canvas, except when she's enjoying a long lunch, which is most of the time.

Dany has become a fashionable overnight sensation and her agent bills accordingly.

She used to use oil paint but switched to acrylics, as she found it much easier to clean her equipment in the local stream. Besides, the toxic materials played havoc with her palmate.

'So how on earth did you get this gig, Narrator?' the Emperor asked.

'It's a funny one.' Narrator chuckled. 'I had to laugh.'

'Why?' Antagonist chipped in. 'Was it in the contract?'

Narrator ignored the comment. 'It goes back to when I was at school.'

'Doesn't everything?' Antagonist said.

Narrator persisted. 'My English teacher [who happened to be Irish] was a right git. I didn't read much in those days, which is why he made an example of me and greatly enjoyed shaming me in front of my classmates.

'"'Narrator, come up here. You're useless,'" he used to say. "You'll never make a name for yourself in literature – or any other type of English, for that matter. You are completely incapable of forming cohesive thoughts, let alone putting sentences with any meaning onto paper. Your words and you are a complete waste of white space."

'I did read a little, but mostly looked through comics and cartoons. It gave me some pleasure and was a little source of pride to demonstrate I had a working knowledge of proverbs, quotations, sayings and put-downs. I was Shaw of my ground.

Standing in front of the form I would silently mouth the words "Those who can, do", and let my classmates finish the quote in unison.

'It was only fair to put the git in his rightful place.

'Looking back, I'm quite happy with the way things turned out, although I guess he was right in a minor sense; funnily enough, I'm not perfect. My trait is that I do ramble occasionally. Part of it is natural, but mainly I put it down to never having worked with an editor. I find it fun to round out a story – not to exaggerate what happened – because truth is often so much stranger than fiction. I was going to mention something relevant here but I'll come back to it later, if I remember.

'Besides, it's also part of my job description to embellish storytelling, adding more layers increases the entertainment value. I like to think of myself as the model model of modern narrator.

'To explain further, I also get paid by the word,' Narrator added.

'And to answer your question, Emperor, I know the Author.'

The 'thing' came down as if everyone were slowly awakening from a bad dream. And over the coming interminable days, that short period of semi-consciousness was considered most people's high point.

It went on for so many months, almost years and the 'thing' became the 'norm', as the end did not seem visible – let alone predictable – even using high-powered future binoculars.

That scenario fitted in well with one definition of time in the Empire. No real beginning, no real end, not much fun, just stuff in the middle.

Exploding on the scene at the debutantes' ball in the early new century, Peony Bombette was viewed as one of the brightest stars in the Empire.

An absolute firecracker in her younger days, she was blessed with a heavenly face and bright disposition.

Unfortunately, things began to unwind when she found herself standing adjacent to the quiet rocket box and it prematurely erupted on Empire celebration day.

Subsequently, she married the Director of the Gunpowder Lolly Shop – Guido Gunpowder.

She wore her scar as a fashion statement, keeping her own name, as Bombettes are recognised as 'stars, which finish with a small explosion'.

He named his most popular firework 'Peony' after her – as sign of love, lust and a tribute to lasting beauty.

Everyone experienced it in her or his own unique way, but the creeping horrors emerged slowly, threateningly.

The Empire seemed unlikely to recover, and if it did, it was unlikely to ever be the same again.

Some thought they'd had the 'thing' before. Some thought they'd never get it. Some thought it never existed in the first place.

The full fears differed but everyone was affected. Symptoms eventuated that were commonly undiagnosable, and the feeling of dread drove everyone into darkness and gloom.

Business stopped. Society stopped. Aeroplanes stopped (some in mid-air). Employment stopped.

Even the weather person took a break.

Everyone started watching cable service. Some speculated that's how you caught it – and it was contagious no matter what channel you tuned into.

Body suits were developed. Breathing apparatus acquired. A few thought dark glasses were the ultimate protection, until the wearers started bumping into fellow disbelievers, even on bright days. Most people buried their heads into their pillows until it was theorised that was the worst thing you could do, as pillows had no natural immunity.

No one knew which way to turn, or what to do, or what not to do.

Those behind the scenes started rubbing their hands.

The news was suspended and the Empire was reduced to such an extent that contemplating navels became the 'in ytnig', or the 'in thing' if you hit the correct keys.

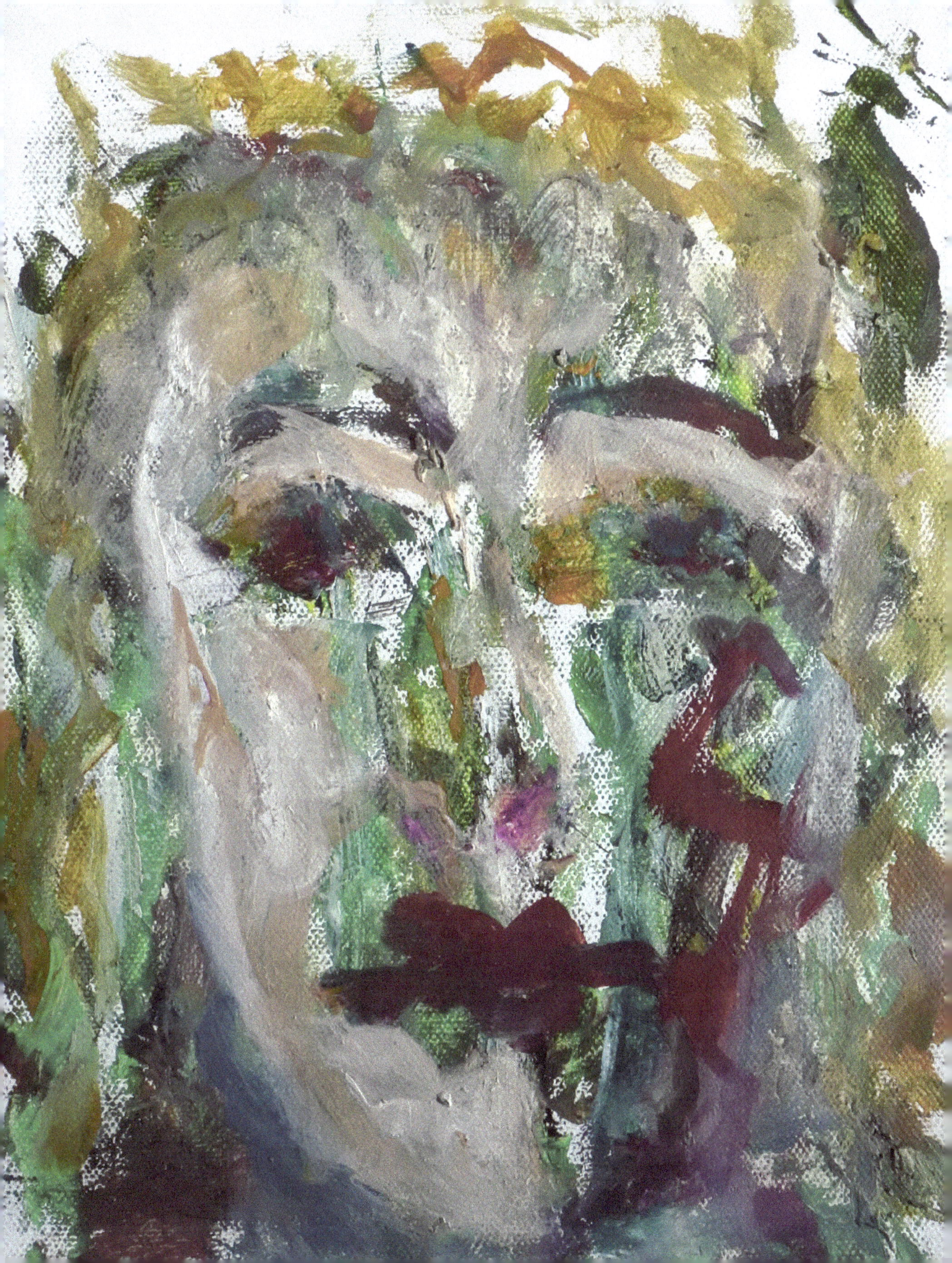

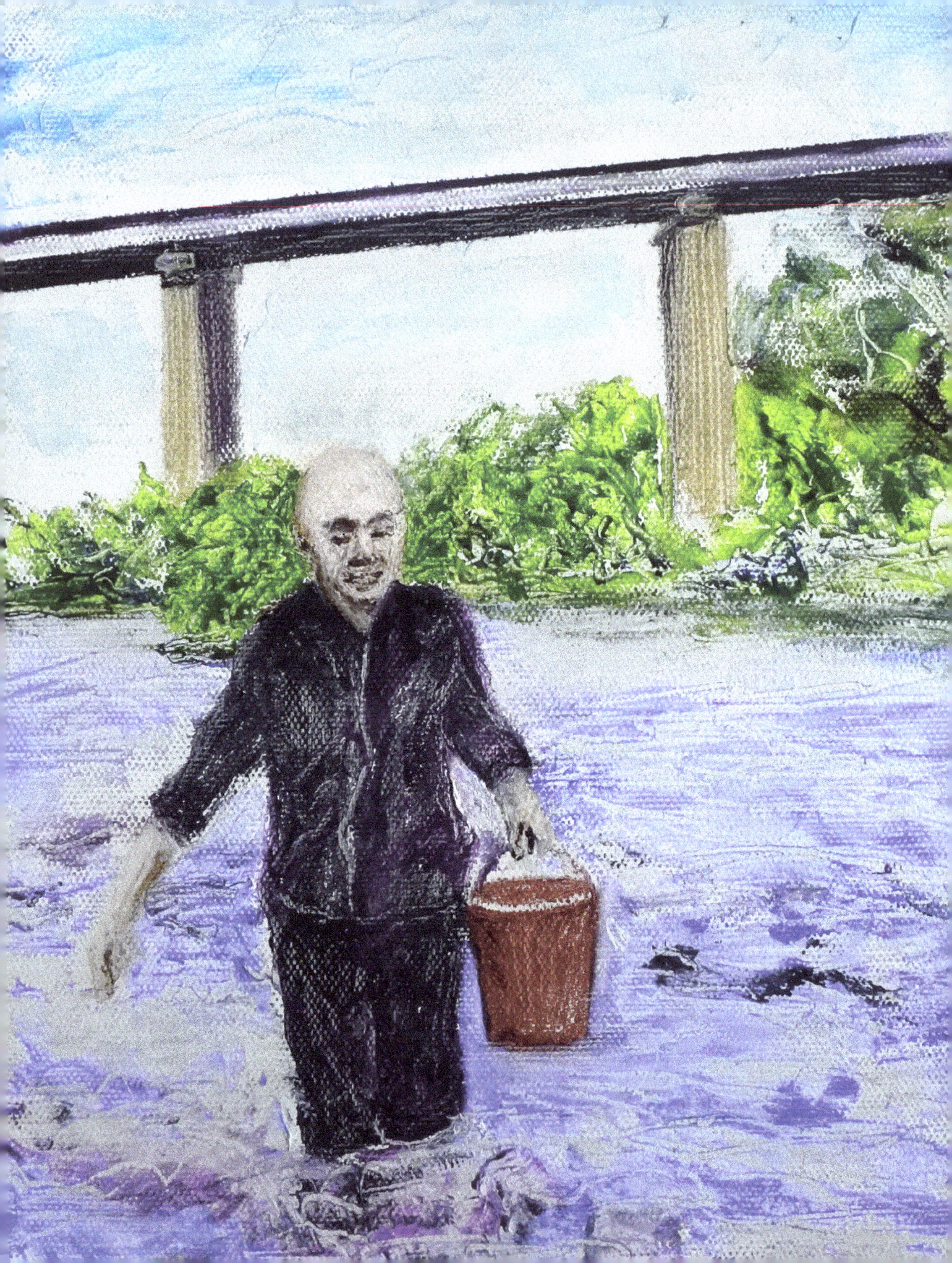

Water finds its own path, but some take enormous pleasure in going against the flow.

As far as belief goes, complete dedication to any 'cause' can be a chastening experience.

Take this dedicated youngster, for example. He was famous for deciding to change the direction of the Esky River, one bucket at a time. This pailed into significance when locals and those from farther afield saw his heroic effort – a metaphor for the struggle required to alter the course of the nondivertable Empire. This then led to forecasting whether (and if) it's possible for a humble citizen (given the right conditions) to assume the ultimate position of power.

Some simply observed it never reigns but it pours.

Social conspiracies abounded, rebounded then slid ever so slowly down the wall accompanied by a clichéd soundtrack of tweeting birds and raucous canned laughter. Picking themselves up, dusting themselves off and adjusting their collective collars, they headed out into the night, fully prepared to pick up and infect the gullible where they left off.

People you thought you knew and assumed were sensible, clear-minded and level headed started to seem the opposite.

Some thought it was a desperate conspiracy to deflect attention from the Empire. 'How's the Empire going?' was deemed to be unthoughtful, unhelpful and downright uncaring. 'How's your wife, husband, kids, friends and relations, cat, dog or hamster?' was deemed appropriate behaviour whilst socially distancing and not communicating with anyone from the supposed safety of your garret. The sky was still blue but it didn't feel that way.

Conspiracy? How could it not be? No one died, but businesses went to the wall.

People stopped seeing people, started hoarding the unimaginable, and toothpicks.

Shelves cleared. Minds fogged.

Writers started writing. Artists started arting.

Bookshops closed and galleries two (both of them).

Was this the reset that was so badly needed?

Power off. Shut down. Black screens.

Silence.

Cooling fans cease.

Tempers rise. Then what?

To those that wanted a different set-up, this was perfect.

The opening stanza had just begun. Orchestrating the full movement was underway.

It was possible the Empire might not be immune after all.

In any branch of society, there are always troublemakers, some of whom are more troublesome than others. Several like to cause ructions anonymously, while others like to make their quarrels public. It's impossible to know how many there are of each, which is why an uncertain proportion of the whole that's easily noticed is generally preferred by the 'authorities' over the remainder, who go unnoticed and slip through attached (or perhaps lumped in with) the unobserved. The completely paranoid and not-so Secret Service (nsSS) made no secret of their intention to find out who was on which side.

It seems almost unbelievable there was a period when the Empire economy was less buttoned down.

Public money was just that.

Though highly criticised at the time, a large budget was procured to buy Yellow Poles, a revolutionary work that some compared to excess building material.

The people primarily responsible were the Dichotomies – Rob and Rich.

One brother wanted to change their names by deed poll to Deedpoll, thinking that Rob and Rich Deedpoll was far more appropriate than Rob and Rich Dichotomy.

The other was totally opposed.

They were non-identical twins, one an art dealer and the other the Arts Minister.

Perhaps Rob and Rich Cahoots would have been a more appropriate choice.

It may have been job preservation (possible), dedication to the Emperor (highly unlikely) or sheer bastardry (absolute certainty) that drove them forward.

Tightly knotted magenta ties (usually around the necks of 'suspects') became only the start of the process or, as the practitioners termed it, 'the beginning of end game'.

Whatever you think is fair doesn't apply here. Take everything you think is right, and purée it.

The nsSS had quite a few 'marks' in sight.

Peony Gunpowder (née Bombette) became a target, simply due to her last names – both married and maiden. Her best friend, Maude Deco, spread tittle-tattle and was regularly seen in all the right (wrong) places. That is why she became 'noticed' and a 'person of interest'.

Peony was always seen on the arm of her husband, Guido Gunpowder (who was also suspected of being an arms dealer), and Maude, who remained distinctly unattached in an 'official' way and unofficially as the consort of young, rich men and women. She often sailed too close to the wind – frequently capsizing in company. Maude's killer looks became of interest too, and the fact she was a single mother, who rejected her only child was completely without morals. She should have got on well with the not-so Secret Service.

Of course, Two-toof was exactly the sort of individual they should have been dealing with, but it emerged that he had changed his name and his political views, starting off on the extreme left before adopting extreme righteousness. He hadn't altered his bullying habits much since his youth but had become rather more sophisticated than 'Take your glasses off'. Mind you, he circulated in high company for a while by marrying the Emperor Mother. That put the undercover operatives in a rather 'sticky position'. EM bit her lip and acknowledged her recent poor choice. She wasn't just unlucky in love.

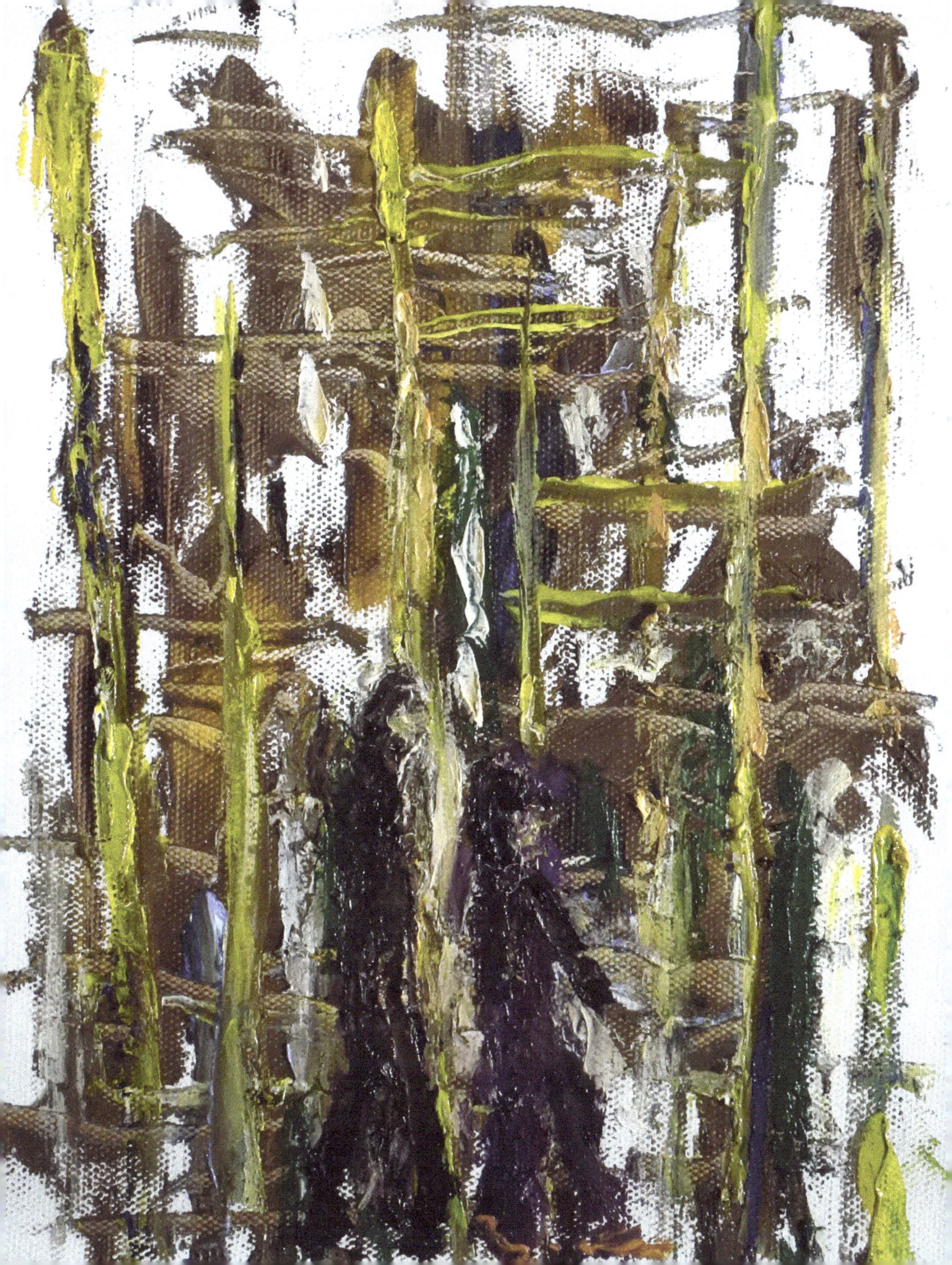

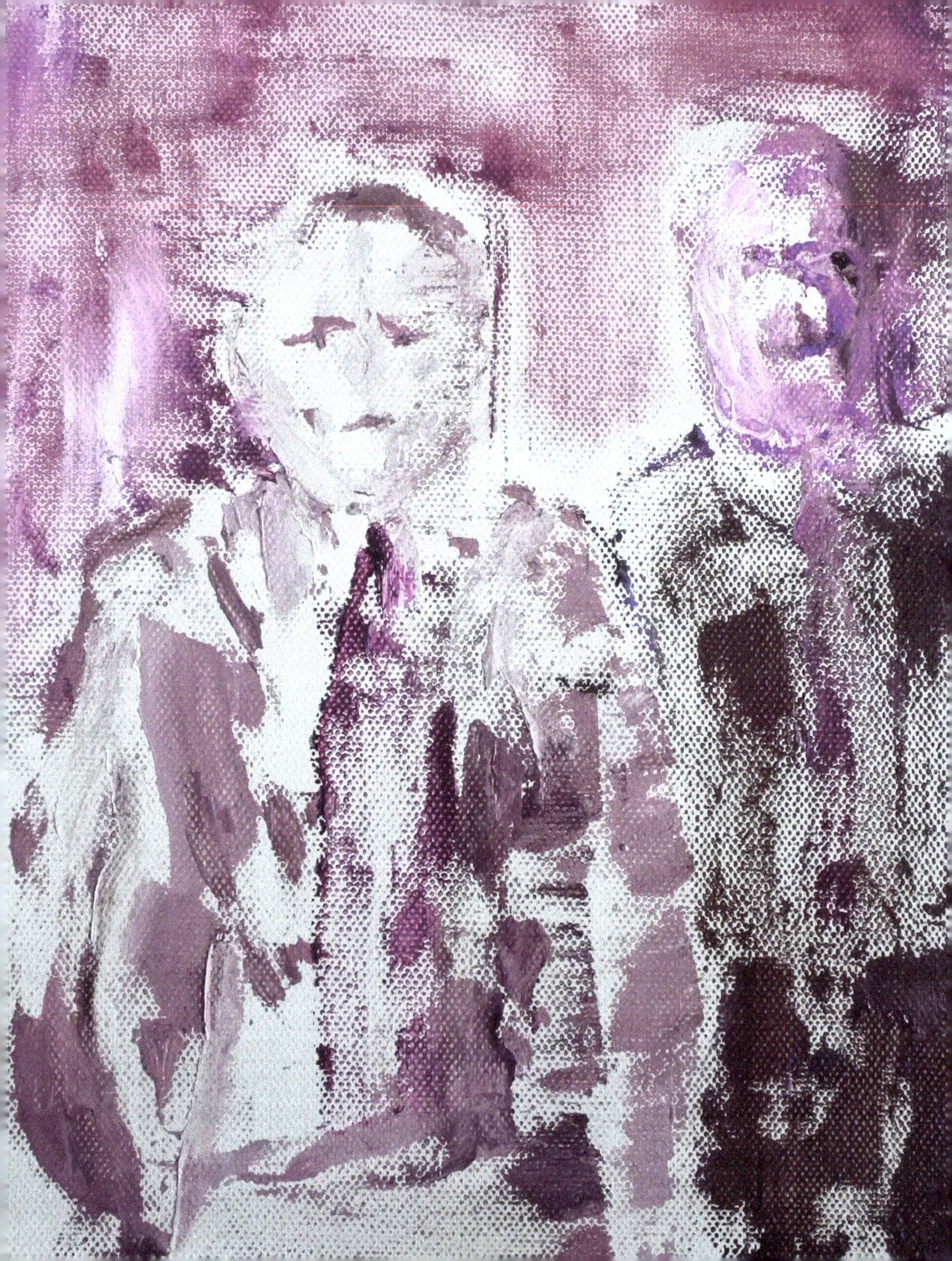

Killing was definitely on their menu.

Diet was not something they contemplated without leaving out the 't'.

You could tell by their tightly tied magenta ties – occasionally with a Windsor, but more often than knot with Reef or Hangman's.

The last was always a deadset clue.

'We'd like to have a little chat with you...' was their favourite refrain. Most people refrained.

If trouble was brewing (and it often was where these two were concerned), as self-appointed members of the appropriately named 'not-so Secret Service', they generally went far beyond their call of duty.

They revelled in the firing line, and especially when anyone stepped out of their definition of 'line'.

EM deserved a lot better. In fact two lots.

Mind you, she had a consistent track record.

She hated every house she currently called home, but loved the one she'd just moved from.

Now where to start with the 'A' lister?

That rhetorical question sits well in present company.

Changing the subjects, there are a few other notables on their short list.

The Dichotomies – Rob and Rich come to mind, but proving maladministration was particularly problematic. The main case was especially difficult to prove since Yellow Poles had massively increased attendance at the Empire Gallery before the 'thing' raised its ugly head.

Yellow Poles created enormous public controversy and its value had increased incrementally due to its growing notoriety.

It was a brilliant buy in the first place and Rob Dichotomy was appointed sole agent for its sale.

Yellow Poles sold for multiple (and I mean multiple!) times its purchase price to a hedge fund.

Of course, Rob shared the commission with his brother under the table.

Part of the proceeds (a minuscule proportion) bought a few drinks for the not-so Secret Service operatives and they quickly lost all prosecutorial interest, whilst looking forward to attending the Empire Gallery's frequent openings and the renowned end-of-year shindig.

The brothers were becoming known as the 'Social Dichotomies'.

Narrator is far more sociable than me, thought the Emperor. He's the type who likes getting together with people. I reckon he goes for coffee most mornings to catch up with friends – probably a small circle but there are many more with whom he's on nodding acquaintance.

With a world of knowledge around that table, they'd exchange stories and laugh, although one of them might complain that Narrator was keeping him from doing the crossword and another that he was stopping him drawing. It would be tongue in cheek, but great fun.

I hope you never have to meet the jailer at work in person. His reputation precedes him and his personal diarised encounter reports usually start with 'I slapped him… but in a real nice way.' He is the man who opens a door and plants an atmosphere, before habitually planting one on his new guest/s. Things generally go downhill from there. Luckily, all types of corporal punishment were restricted to the lower ranks of the armed services. Unluckily, this was a military facility, and if you weren't ranked, you qualified for the spa treatment, though these types of places don't have a spa. So customarily it was a full body treatment instead.

'It wouldn't happen on the northside of Anonymity.' The Emperor lamented. 'That's the cultural wasteland… without the culture.'

Narrator naturally brings people together, whereas I am unable, he thought. It wasn't that he was an outcast; after all, he was the Emperor. It was as though he felt he didn't really belong in the present, or, for that matter, any company.

'Can I ask you a question, Emperor?'

'Don't you mean can I ask two questions?'

'No,' replied Narrator.

'Well, you've already asked me one.'

'Oh, I see. Okay then.' *Literal so-and-so*, thought Narrator.

(Here Narrator added: *Actually I didn't think 'so-and-so' but frown on very bad language – particularly in print. My apologies for continually referring to myself in the third person. It's a very bad trait, which I picked up from reading quotes from sportspeople in print media. However, the Author should not have placed me in such an insidious and uncomfortable position from the opening paragraph.)*

The Emperor grinned. It was one of his favourite ripostes.

He was continually surprised that so many people asked the completely unnecessary first 'non-question'.

'Here's the second. How long have you felt this way?'

'What way?'

'That you're an outsider.'

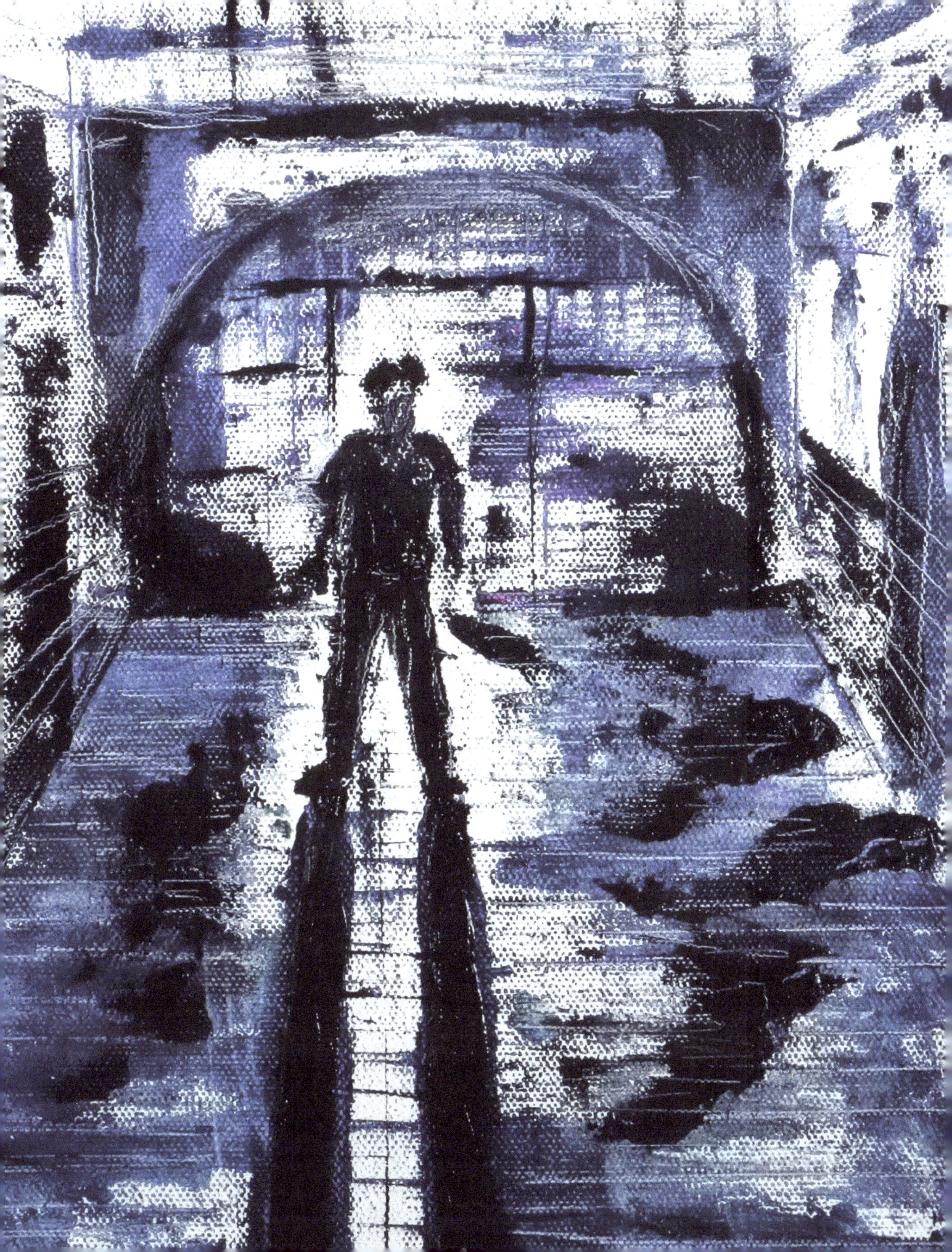

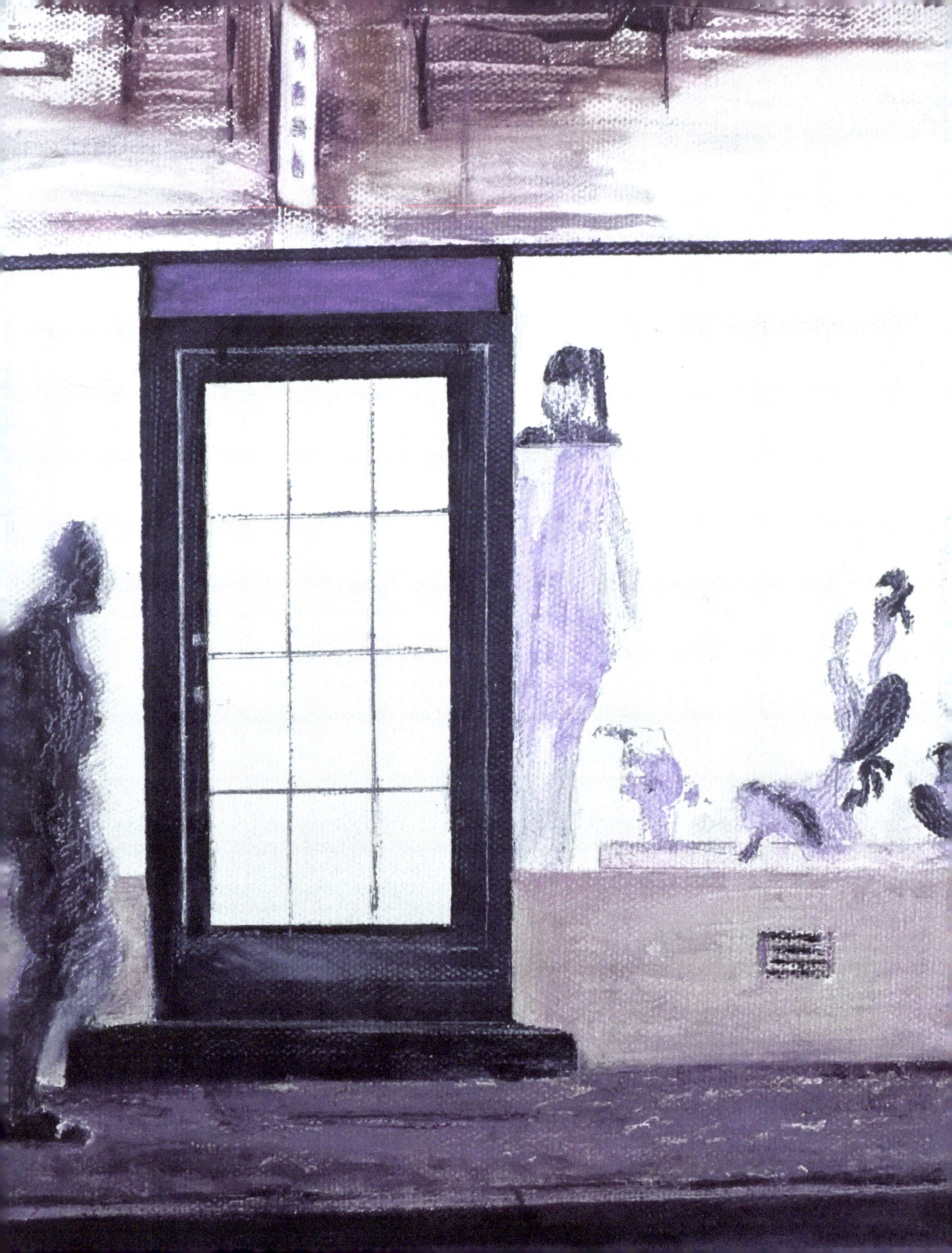

It was nearing dusk and the visual merchandiser thought she might have seen him – but she wasn't sure.

Annette Curtain was unqualified to make the call, as her job (though she was on the inside) was all about looking in from the outside, not looking out from the inside.

She thanked her privilege, because others who worked for Measley and Pittance always had to make their own way to these assignments carrying everything they needed – props, plants, mannequins, tools and all manner of eye-catching devices.

Her favourite was a poster that proclaimed, 'Our wines is dry, our English is pour...' and her least favourite: 'Counterfeit, can't be beat'.

She's aware that in retail, and across the Empire, the only constant is change.

I hate that sort of question... How long this? How long that? How long did it take you to write that book? How long did it take you to paint that picture? It's irrelevant how long it took and it shouldn't matter. Just look at the end result and assess that.'

'Sorry to upset you,' said Narrator.

'I'm not upset. I'm just losing patience. My preferred answer to that type of question is how long I've been able to think. I'm saying look at the results of that knowledge, not how long the outcomes took. It's like asking me how long it takes to boil the perfect egg. The answer is the same... no, it's not four or five minutes! It's years, even decades.'

'Well, I doubt that. I think it would be rather overcooked, and you would ruin the pot. The water would boil dry! You might even destroy the kitchen.'

'No, Narrator – this is what I mean. It's the gaining of experience that's important. It is non-transferrable, because it's self-contained. You can't teach a person experience. You can only help them acquire knowledge. The rest is what they pick up and do with what they've learned. A perfect boiled egg can take more than 50 years. Some never learn it. It's like being able to pick the perfect avocado.'

'Now I know what you mean,' replied Narrator. 'That's something I still get wrong as often as I get it right. And you don't know the outcome until you've cut it open. And by then it's too late to do anything about it.'

'Bang on. Now you see my point. Some stuff happens, and no matter how much you know, or what you've achieved or what position you're in, you are simply guessing the outcome. That's why asking how long it took is irrelevant. It's almost as bad as asking the "non-question" in the first place.'

'I promise not to do that again,' said Narrator, who had begun to feel rather chastened.

'Well, to actually answer your question – the second one, not the first – I've felt this way as long as I can remember...'

With that the Emperor took his leave.

Narrator went for a coffee.

To meet with his friends in Till & Boni's.

The Emperor considered bringing in laws to outlaw anti-social behaviour. But since he didn't have any friends (not the human ones anyway), he had no real understanding of the issues.

Social media. More like antisocial media, if you ask me,' thought Narrator. *You meet online, do your new 'friends' the favour they requested. Then they cease responding or unfriend you. Not a lot of gratitude there. Get a LifeBook.*

A remarkable man, Dun Diminutive continually defied every reasonable expectation of anyone's normal capabilities. Dun simply wouldn't be defined by other people's limited vision. He therefore acquired the epithet 'Can'.

Legally blind, Can didn't use conventional methods of recognition.

In previous times of calm he led the pact to became a shining light in the face of the approaching storm.

Here Can is pictured on Crater Island as one of the first to explore the new landmasses – again demonstrating his remarkable capabilities.

Can is a brilliant example of how it's frequently possible for the blind to lead the sighted – truly a case of not just can but do.

He also saw right through the Emperor.

These people are similar to those who choose to be unpleasant to make an unnecessary point when they could just as easily be nice. For some reason they get untold (wish it were) pleasure in being disagreeable and even go out of their way to do so. Inflicting yourself on others should be outlawed. First offence would warrant public airing on the community noticeboard. Second and subsequent occasions, the offenders' stocks would be further reduced – preferably by spending some time in them, in the town square.

Another of his oft-observed 'needless stupidity' hates was ignorant, uncaring drivers overtaking on the inside of the highway. He referred to the practice as undertaking, because it was a short cut for a fast trip to the undertaker (albeit it in what's supposed to be the slow lane). Either way, the person in front never saw it coming until they'd collected their one-way ticket to the local cemetery (which is often referred to as the dead centre of town). It's amazing what blind spots contain. They are packed full of unexpected unseens, lying in weight.

Keep left unless overtaking, you dumb nut (or right if you happen to be in those countries with steering wheels on the left.). What's so hard to understand about that? Oh, the speed limit, road rules and common sense don't apply to you. Wrong again. Sorry. The first two do, the third doesn't.

And don't get the Emperor started on unnecessarily noisy motorbikes, cyclists with attitude (sorry, needless thought duplication) in body-hugging material (more superfluity) and food delivery drivers on two wheels. They should have their own lane named Fast Track to Hell Lane.

Collectively, they are an arsehole without buttocks. Have a good look at yourselves, you individual one-eyed orifices.

'Don't hold back, Emperor. Tell us what you really think,' suggested Narrator.

The Emperor always felt better having vented. Sometimes he didn't feel like holding back.

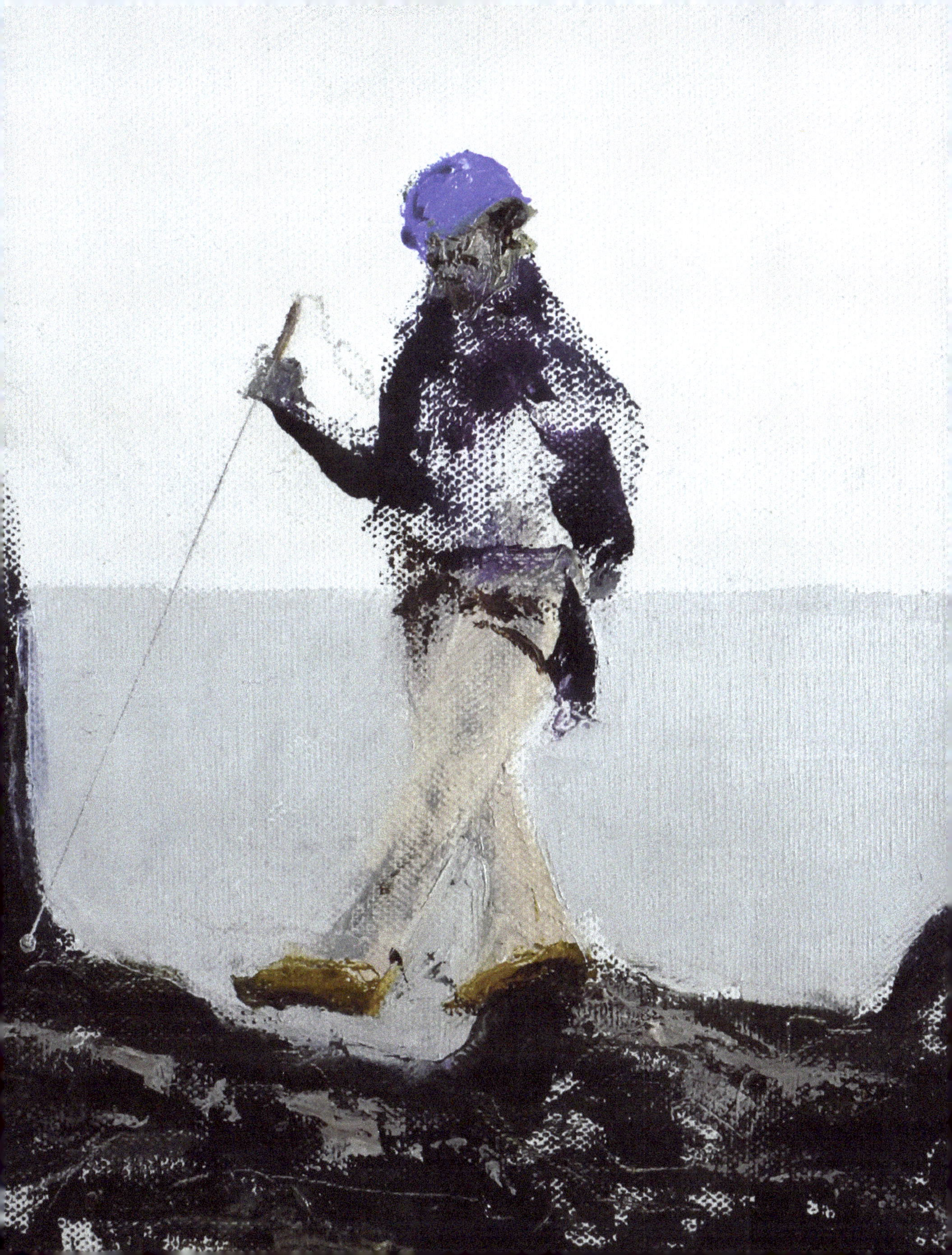

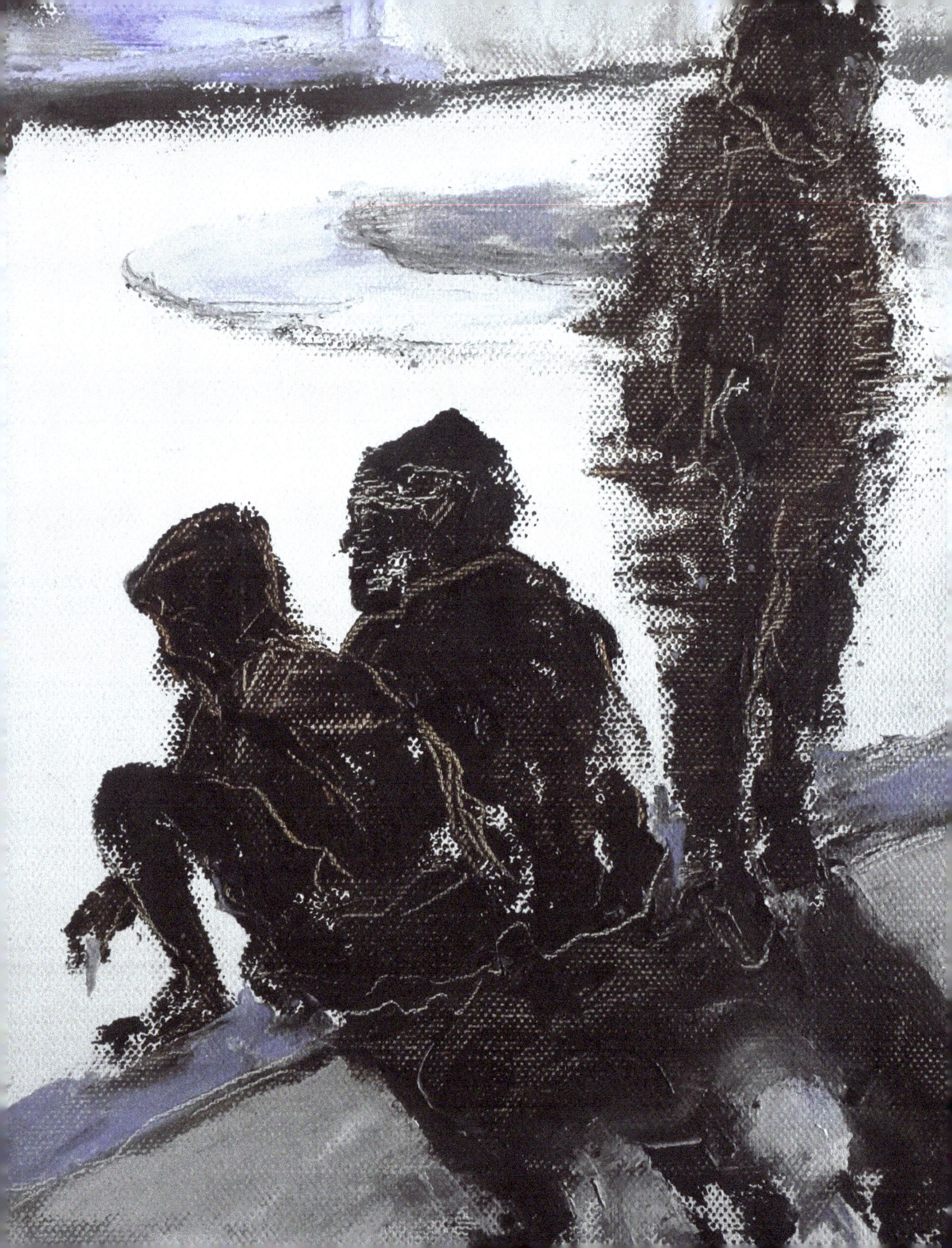

Night-time was when the young ones used to meet to discuss the current state of play near the traffic calming devices. Even in their youth, they appreciated the irony. Too young to drive and too young to vote, they knew their time was fast approaching and everything would be different in the future. That's called hereditary optimism. What they didn't know, they didn't know – but there would be plenty of time to catch up, and with what had gone down, they knew they were up and coming. When they ran out of motivation they'd often catch the midnight train to nowhere in particular. It wasn't a round trip, neither cyclical or circular. They were waiting for their time to shine, in a roundabout way.

They knew it was about time.

The 'thing' kept popping up just when you thought it was on its way out. Like the last guest at the house parties that used to be organised without thinking, and who never took the hint that it was time to go. It just hung around stubbornly and didn't even help with the clearing up.

Nonetheless, even in deep space, you could only have tables of ten...

This had a wearing effect on morale.

When you're effectively locked up domestically, there's a fair bit of time to think.

It's no reflection on you, but when there's no one else around, the mirror is always the obvious place to start the criticism. When that monologue becomes exhausting (after all, you have to play all the parts), the focus naturally shifts.

The Empire was noticeably becoming more 'on the nose' and there really wasn't anywhere else to look to shift the blame.

People started wondering what the future held.

Some even speculated that the future was a long way off.

Not everyone played by the rules – which is what the 'thing' looked for.

The thing was that the 'thing' had a levelling effect.

Take the Emperor, for example. The duties of the top job came before any personal choices and it was amongst the biggest downside to the ultimate position of power. It wasn't just duty that held him back. He found it difficult to have normal aspirations but his position was no longer unique. Nowadays there were no-go places for everyone.

It just didn't seem just.

Eating out, going to the theatre, the ballet, the beach or the footy were all things he would have enjoyed, like so many others. No matter how hard he tried, the Emperor didn't take to the opera (but let's not make a performance about that). The activities list was pretty well endless. Everything was affected. He even considered 'going to the snow', as he preferred colder weather and always found it easier to get warm when cold than it was to get cool when you were hot.

He would have liked to try skiing (although he knew he'd be no good).

Canines they were. A pigeon pair they were not. How they became the most well-recognised dogs in the Empire deserves pause for thought.

According to his biographer, the Emperor let his thoughts run wild at the Rorschach Puppy Farm. He was looking to buy a Mountain Dog, considered to be highly suitable for a man in his position. After much deliberation and some soul searching, he left with a pair of Dalmatians. Although from the same litter, they were complete opposites.

One was Tops, the other spoT.

This reveals much about the Emperor's personality, psyche and thought process.

It's said he was not decisive – because he saw both sides of most stories.

Detractors said he couldn't make up his mind, so was doggedly unsuited to his day job.

Some presumed the Emperor was either a Gemini, or Libran.

Others didn't believe in astrology.

This was just the tip of the iceberg.

Being in his position felt like a slippery slope.

It used not to seem fair. But nowadays nearly everyone was in the same boat.

Yes, it was a big boat, I hear you thinking (I am Narrator, after all.)

What used to separate the Emperor from the average citizen was normality.

A peculiar effect of the 'thing' was that it actually brought people closer to the Emperor. And when everyone starts thinking the same thing, weird things happen.

It seemed a highly unusual situation and even completely unlikely.

That's why some called the 'thing' a conspiracy and led others to insist that it couldn't possibly exist.

Discord was growing louder.

Disquiet was getting rowdier.

People started looking for something or someone concrete to blame.

Fingers were beginning to be metaphorically pointed.

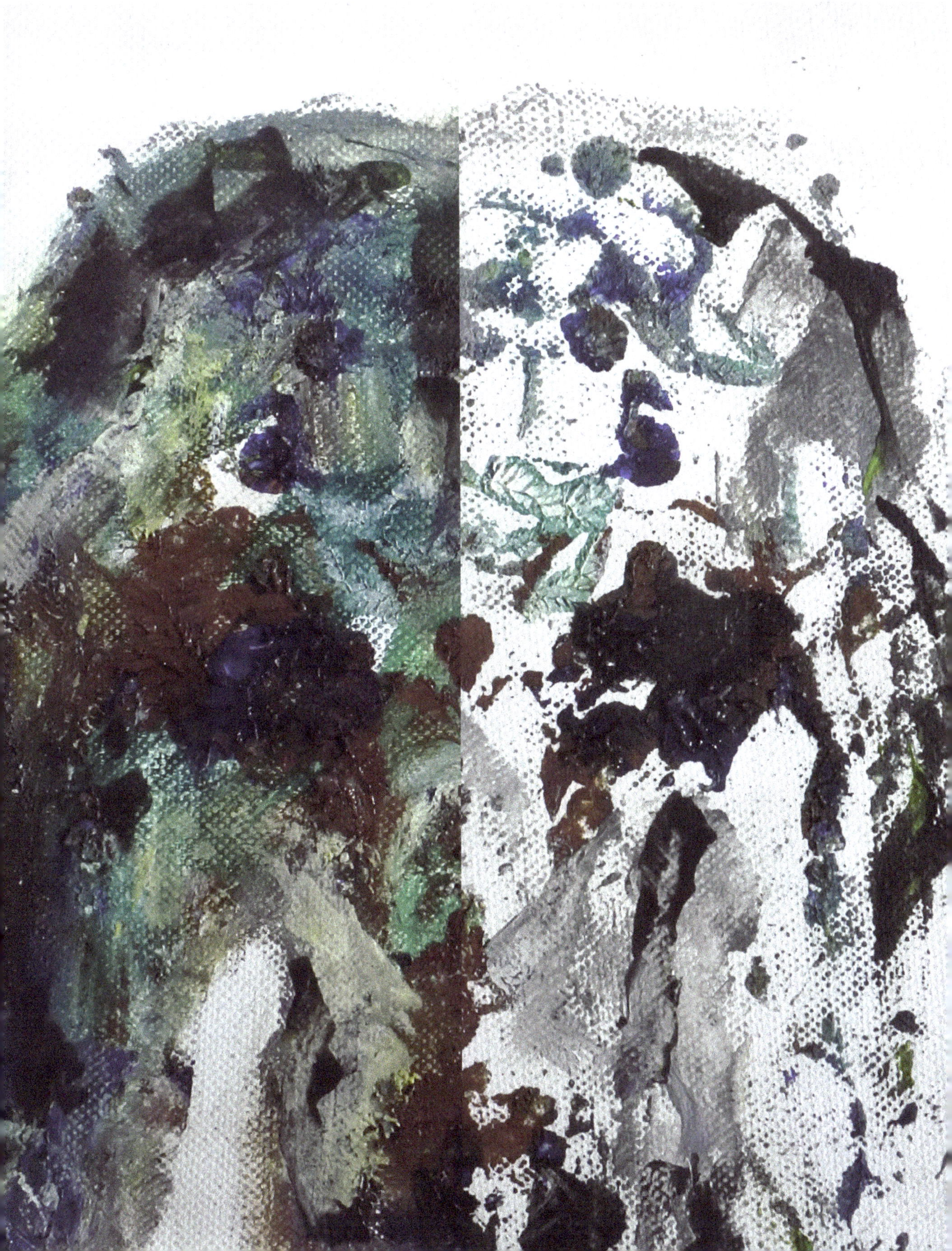

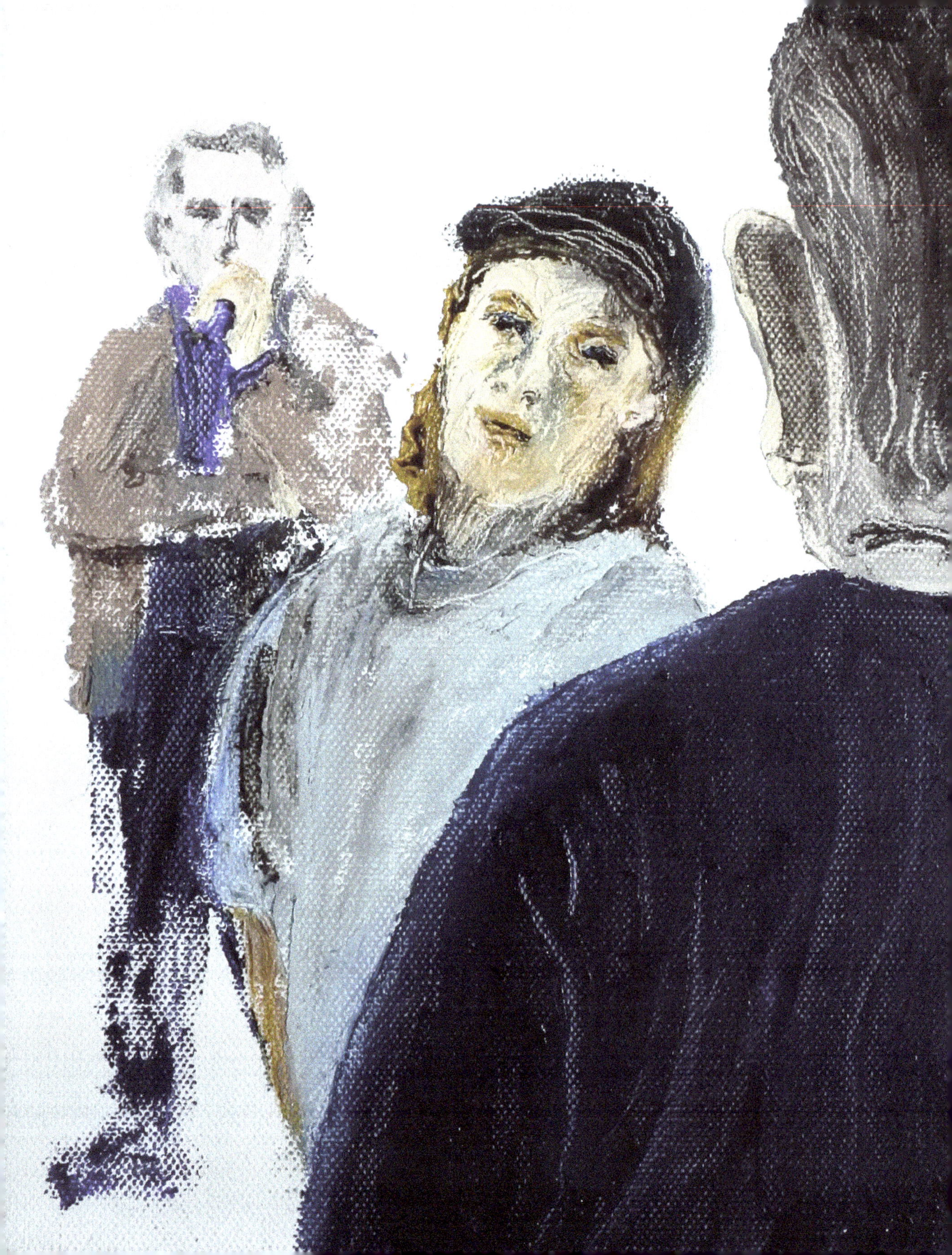

The Court's Jester had one key responsibility. His main role required him to act as both Empire PR man and Minister for Propaganda (specialising in fake news). Basically, he was there to lift the mood of the general population, keep everything 'light' and put a positive spin on even the darkest developments.

Everyone knew you couldn't believe anything he said – or at least a large percentage of it. He was a hard act to follow, so he had the nightly spot on the news after the weather girl.

'Justice must be seen to be done' doesn't apply in the Empire.

Actually, it doesn't even apply in 'real' life.

As you can tell, reality is a difficult concept – particularly where celebrity is concerned.

This 'A' lister was brought in for questioning, and truth be told (which it wasn't), it ended up being more like an evil inquisition.

In the rambling interview, where not one question provided a single intelligible answer, everyone was left utterly confused, which of course was the whole point of the exercise. This personality liked to 'pull the wool' over everyone's eyes. In getting out and about (and out of it too), he didn't mind treading on the toes of authority.

He made enemies in high places, proving sometimes it pays to fly under whichever radar is in power.

One night, a big story emerged via social media (before mainstream picked it up) and the rumour spread like butter on hot toast.

It appeared the Emperor had hacked his own identity and posted his handprint online in a community noticeboard (not very anonymously). It was shared instantly, millions of times, and before anyone realised it, it became impossible to even begin to attempt to track the real Emperor – adding further to his mystique.

His handprint was blocked across the Empire, so he couldn't even access wi-fi, streaming services or his email.

This one act helped cloud his identity totally, assisting him to escape the clutches of his people and the daily duties of his post.

Some bright art student made a poster of the image and sold billions.

Whether true or not, the hacking served one purpose. It perpetuated the mystery surrounding the Emperor. Even though the state of the Empire was diminishing, his popularity increased. Women on the street and men in their ivory towers (other than those who had tried to gain advantage) started to feel sympathetic.

The Emperor became even more ubiquitous.

This was bad news to the few that really mattered – the ones pulling the strings.

We haven't heard much about them so far.

But you should be in the know.

There were dark, anonymous forces plotting against the Emperor.

With all the CCTV cameras around, seemingly hanging from every natural vantage point, or on top of an ugly post planted specifically to create one that didn't exist, the Emperor appeared to avoid regular detection. (There goes the English language disagreeing with itself again – surely he couldn't have evaded all the cameras if he'd appeared.), noted the Brackets.

Yes, there were regular reported sightings but no one could be really sure.

Even with facial recognition technology having improved out of sight (!), in reality, confirmation was virtually impossible.

Palm recognition is the preferred method of providing identity across the Empire.

Unfortunately, it's proved premature.

The Emperor's hacked handprint had been posted on social media, representing a major security breach that would have lasting repercussions in a number of arms of the universal security services and banking monopoly.

Photo recognition was not an option (as nobody knew what the Emperor looked like), so anyone in possession of his pseudo palm printout was in a primary position to proceed in a very underhand way, and probably go unpunished...

There had been a spate of identity thefts and everyone was advised to take a good look at themselves, just in case someone had made off with theirs.

It was a process that the thieves had made their own specialty.

Combined with an utter lack of honesty, assuming someone else's identity was the starting point. The identity burglars then systematically robbed not only assets, but also the victim's dignity and crushingly diminished their reputation.

It was, and continues to be faceless thieving, not victimless crime.

Forewarned, people started locking their rubbish bins, then either misplacing their padlock keys or failing to recall the combination. Most forgot which day their rubbish was collected anyway. So the problem started piling up.

Then disguised operatives began to appear in increasingly large numbers. Purported to be agents of foreign governments, white ibis started going through the accumulating debris looking for evidence of trojan horse machinations within newly contracted plans for 18G communication technologies – a flying squad of compromised futures and potential come what mays... not ifs or butts.

They were expertly probing for evidence and covertly taking off with snippets of personal information.

Most thought they were looking for sustenance... or building material (not to furnish their nests, but) to assemble cases against unnamed, unknowing subversives.

As the rubbish mounted up, the rumours abounded, conspiracy theories overflowed.

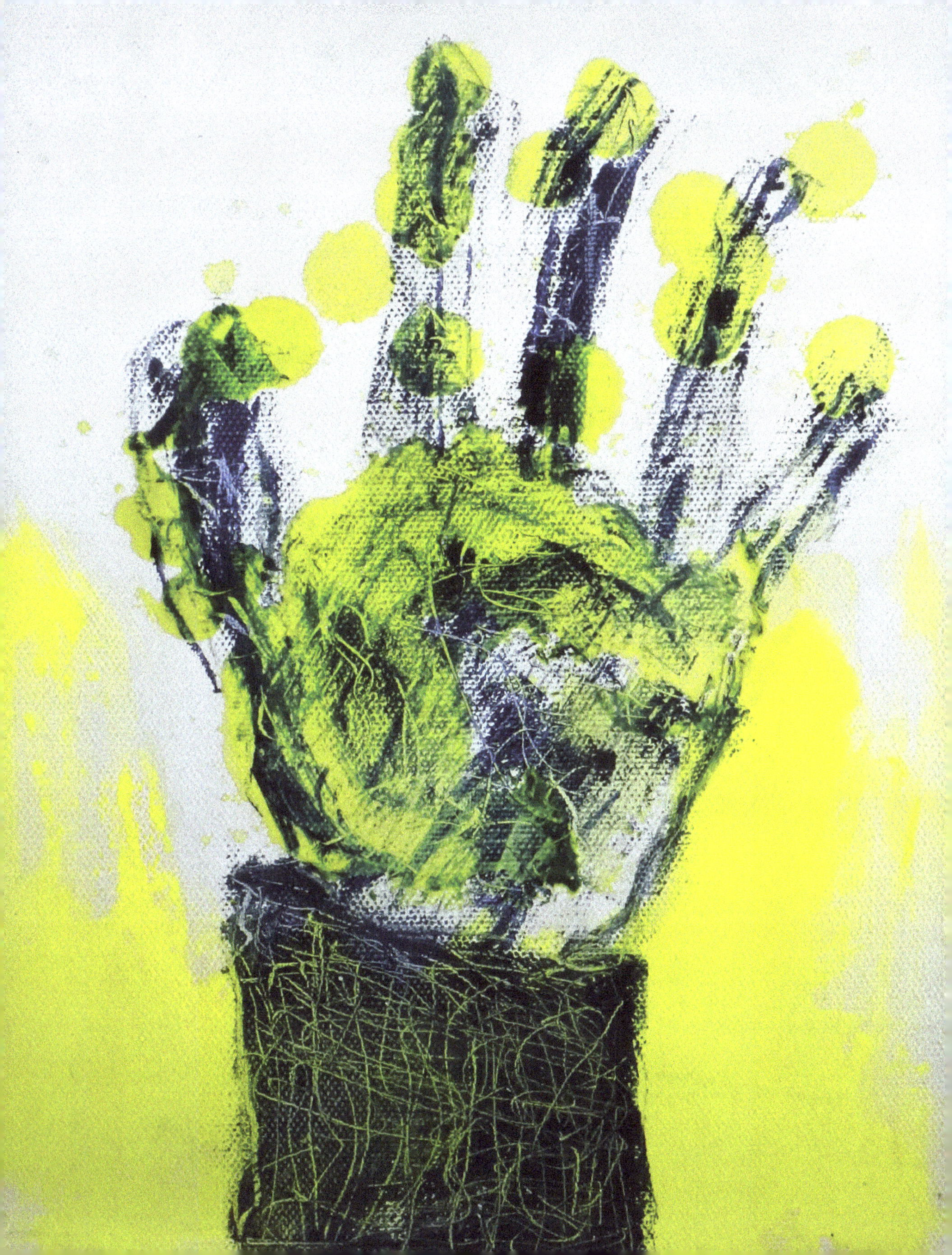

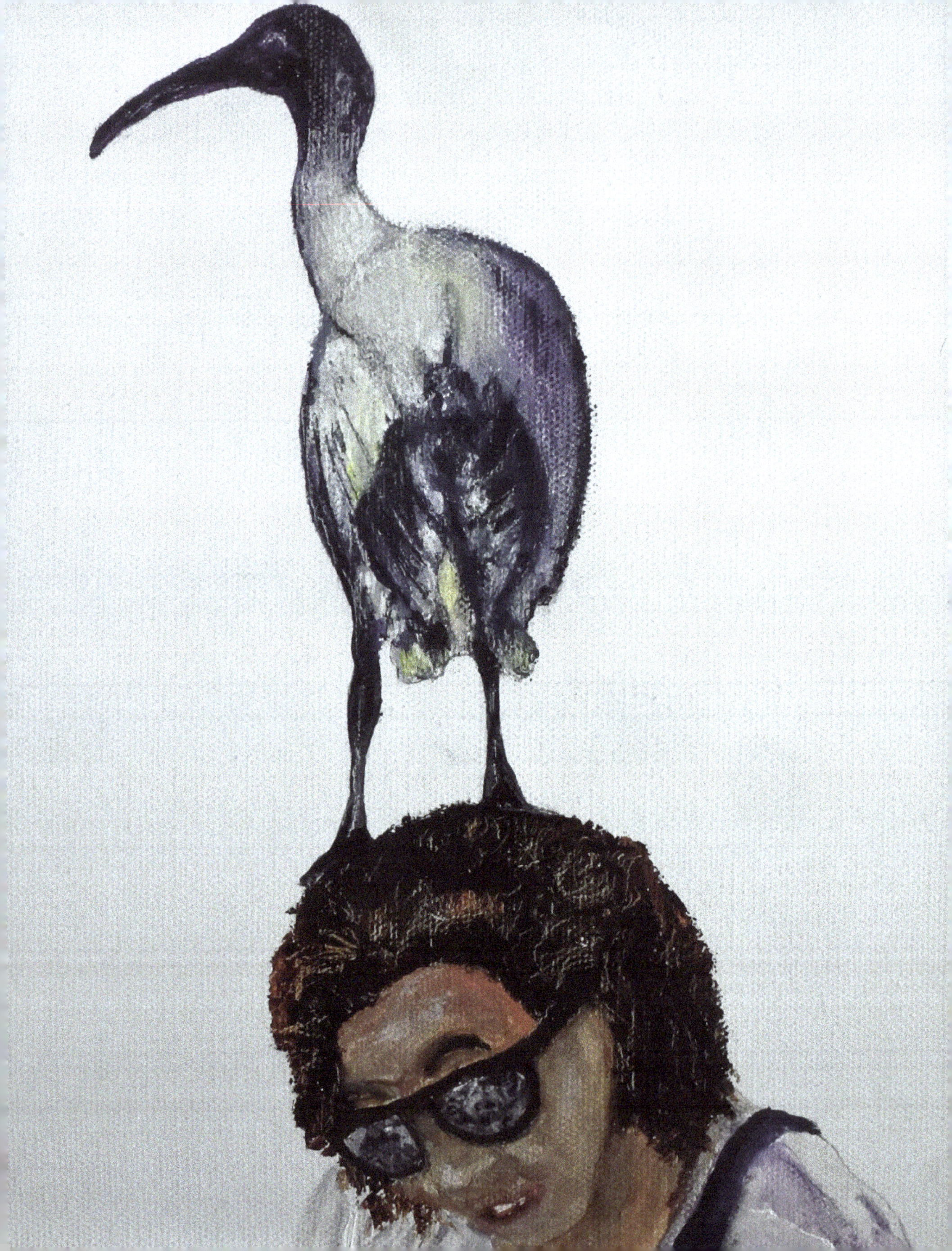

There's something on the nose.

Something's ahead.

This woman is proof of the burden.

It's understood the head ibis licensed their beak design to the largest manufacturer of walking sticks in the Empire, retaining the intellectual property. This provided ibis with vast resources, enabling international travel, superior housing and a life of leisure.

Not wanting to rest on their laurels, they took up fossicking.

Perhaps ibins would be a more accurate name for the species.

You heard it here first – apart from trying to make off with your identity, many thought they were foreign agents, rummaging through unlocked or overflowing rubbish containers, looking for evidence of mobile phone conspiracies... or 'thing' spreading intrigues, or (insert your theory here).

All bets are off.

Bin chickens are ruling the roost.

Bit by bit and piece by piece, these spoon-billed, bandy-legged, fat-arsed felons accumulated material.

The data initially appeared irrelevant and unimportant, until it reached critical mass.

Then a complete identity could be assembled and become legitimised through complete and utter rubbish.

I've met him, alleged Antagonist (referring to the Emperor).

Takes one to know one, thought Retort.

People started becoming paranoid.

It was currently the Empire's state.

The Emperor went on another short trip to the country.

He'd been to the estate a long time ago but only as a day visitor, taking a short excursion away from the main purpose of his trip – when he found he had a few hours spare in his busy schedule.

This time he took the quiet country back road and visited the place that had been left to the Empire by a well-credentialled, generous benefactor from a previous period of existence.

These days, across the Empire, it's a fact that killer looks help you fly. This woman is taking that adage to a serious new level. Amongst twitchers, she has high hopes to become the best in the business and is using her skills to rapidly make her way up society's scaffold – building a nest egg by fair means or fowl. She is certainly not cuckoo (although she is pushing her young one out). In making that call, her notoriety follows, because she naturally knows how to stand out in a crowd (which is not helpful for a birder). Her plumage is also a dead giveaway, but as far as elegance goes, she's first edition.

Meet Maude Deco – on the hunt for opportunities to further feather her nest.

There were strings attached to the gift, but the estate (located near a beautiful, meandering river) comprised a traditional home and various outbuildings, including one that had been the original kitchen. (In those days, due to fire hazards, the cooking facilities were separate from the main house.) Other buildings included a multitude of workshops – one that had an enormous traditional brick kiln and another with a lathe, which was used to produce the chunky turned legs on the massive, stunningly beautiful, weathered wooden furniture in the main house.

From time to time over the years, the river level had risen substantially, but the house was located a good distance from the normal watercourse and well above the flood plain. Once, 100 years earlier, the water had lapped the bottom step of the house but had gone no further.

Generations of the family lived on the estate, often cohabiting across decades and marriages. Even though centuries of farming and husbandry were the primary sources of the family's wealth, writers, painters, potters and sculptors pursued their various vocations. The family had hearts of art.

The buildings, their contents, the land and myriad fine works were indeed a generous and lasting present for the public good.

Nowadays, the estate was used for education, residencies and field trips and the valley looked very different.

On his original visit, the Emperor (who was of course in mufti and unrecognisable) spotted a small, strange-looking chimneyed structure nestled into the tree line.

When back in Anonymity, he researched the history of the area and found the building was originally called the Solitary Fella Shelta.

He felt he needed to find out more.

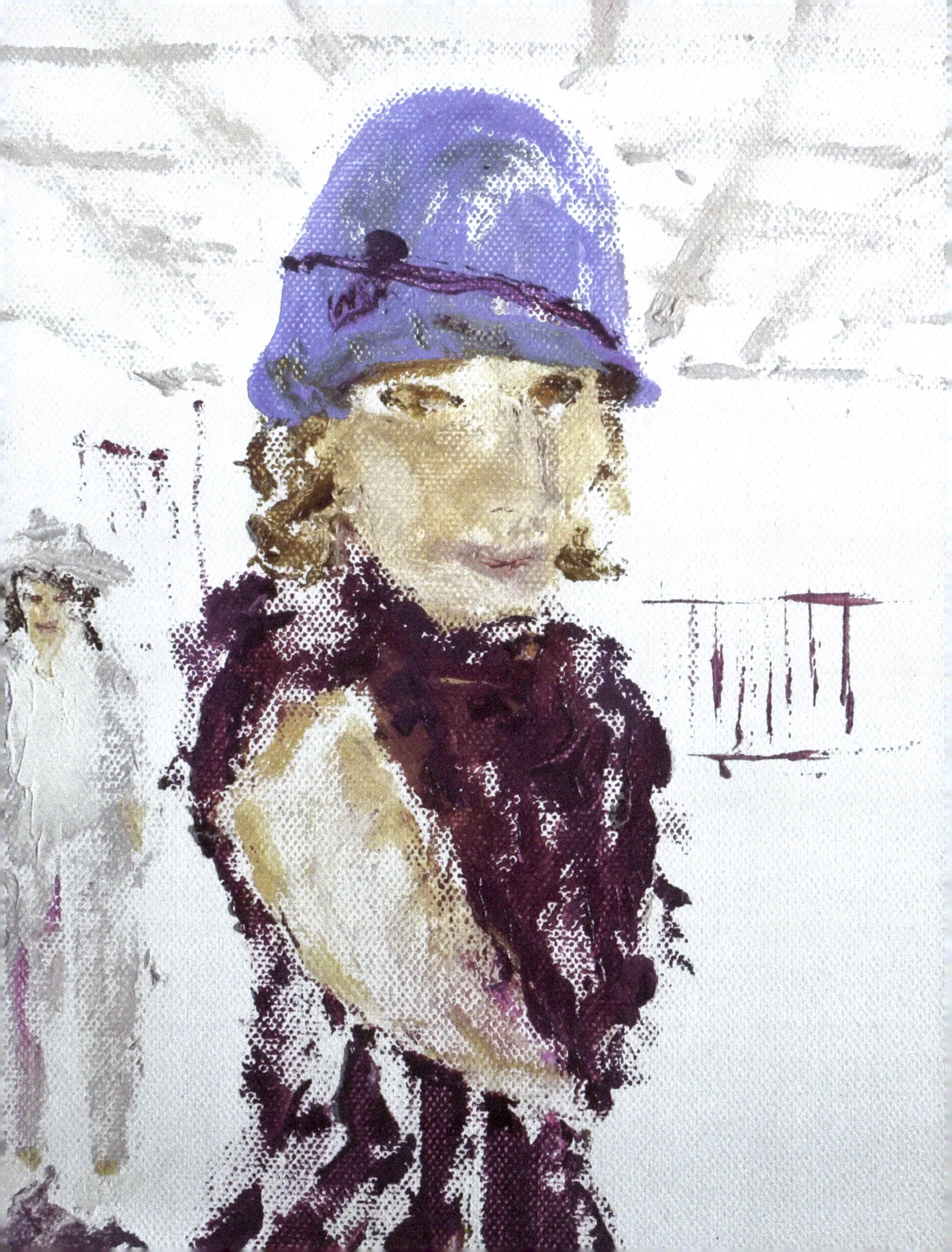

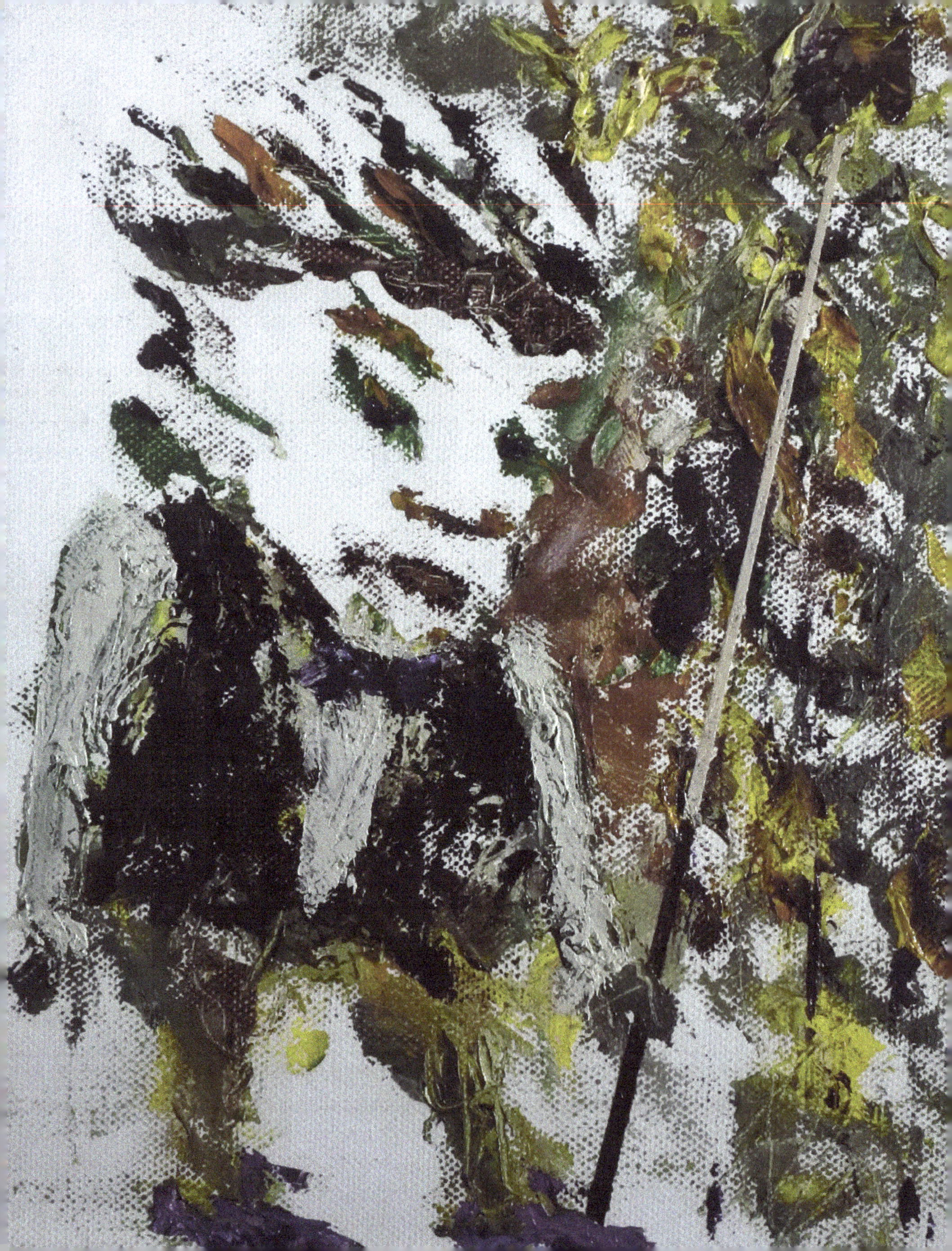

Known as 'King of Tables', the goblin Joachim surfaced as a renowned snooker and eight-ball player.

Although his talent wasn't inherited from the immediate members of his family, it must have existed in the genetic cesspool from whence he emerged.

It wasn't just his childhood he wasted.

Throughout his career, he had the habit of not just beating his opponent but chewing their heads off too.

Short legs were his biggest hindrance, as he had to play every shot with a rest, a spider, swan, half butt or occasionally a full butt.

He took his fashion cues and flamboyance from his namesake – the King of Naples.

People wondered if he could possibly be the Emperor.

Little did they know.

This time, the main reason for the Emperor's trip was to inspect the seemingly derelict structure across the valley.

The Emperor considered the building and its location to be a good analogy for the way he felt, thinking, *I'm like an open book; I have no guile. No matter how hard I try, my innermost thoughts are on permanent display. Regardless of how much I attempt to conceal my feelings, there is simply nowhere to hide. Like this hut, I am just there – standing still – for all to see.*

Devoid of deviousness, and ruing his gullibility, the Emperor made his way towards it across the fields. From his viewpoint, the house's construction was difficult to make out. Why did it look that way?

A fireplace appeared to be the wrong way round, facing outwards. If you lit a fire there, it would serve no logical purpose. It was inside out.

As he got closer, he realised half the building was missing. The original design made use of a single chimney, splitting near the apex of the roofline, with back-to-back hearths.

Due to the direction of his approach, he could only see what appeared to be an end wall – and the stonework of the apparently nonsensical hearth. It made no sense as an exterior wall (which is what it now was) but as he got closer, the Emperor realised it was originally designed as an internal partition. It needed the other three walls to make it a room, and they were now absent.

He walked around the stone end wall and along the portion of the building that was left. All the other walls were timber – old and ancient timber that had weathered grey.

These standing walls were entirely constructed of short, hand-hewn planks with a small window on each side and a door at the end.

A slight floating porch with slanted roof provided a little protection and the entire structure was essentially a simple wooden box propped above the ground level on a series of large stones.

There was a sloping tin roof, the colour of rust. The process of decay was obvious.

The Emperor marvelled at the desolate hut's exterior – the effect though rustic was uncharacteristically sculptural.

The Emperor was unaware that Joachim was the last inhabitant of the Solitary Fella Shelta.

The space inside was just big enough for a snooker table, so the goblin slept on the floor beneath it.

He had no need of the fireplace (inside or out), as he ate his food raw… always fresh, and usually still warm.

Joachim used the 'up ladder' sleeping platform as an area for his clothes – particularly his collection of multicoloured embroidered waistcoats, and finest handwoven shirts with padded shoulders and ruffs to tease the referees and his growing band of fans.

It's said that prodigious talent on the snooker table is a sign of a misspent youth.

This goblin spent nothing… he always called his time on the tables his free time.

But for his opponents, it ended up costly.

Holding his hand to the glass to minimise reflections, he peered through the small windows.

The bubbles, distortions and discolouration of the old crystal – and the small amount of light the panes let through – made the interior difficult to make out.

The Emperor stepped on to the veranda and moved towards the door. It was off-centre and made for someone of much smaller stature. An old wooden latch was all that kept the door from swinging open. Lifting the handle, the Emperor pulled the door open and walked inside.

The smell wasn't what he'd expected. It wasn't dusty or musty. The scent was of cedar. The interior wooden walls looked different from the planks on the exterior. Slimmer, better finished and protected from the elements, in the half-light, they projected a warm, satiny glow.

The interior was a single room with a wide ladder up to a platform where the former occupants would have slept. At the end, opposite the door, the mirror-image stone hearth would have been used to not only heat the space but for cooking. The wooden floor was protected from the fire by a large stone surround and the floorboards were the same bleached grey as the outside – but from countless years of mopping, not daylight from the nearest three stars.

All the Emperor could hear was the wind in the trees, birds calling from across the valley and a nearby frog that sounded like a tennis rally. He could so easily imagine that this was the perfect home he'd envisaged but had never possessed. Let's see what the future holds.

In his mind he pondered a fitting description – half there, half not and with one side of the interior half exposed, an analogy for his inner feelings.

A name came almost immediately.

'The Emperor's Retreat' resounded strongly.

He had found the perfect location and the ideal premises.

Now all he needed was time to set up an unimpeachable premise to walk away from the job – leaving behind him the weight of his countless responsibilities.

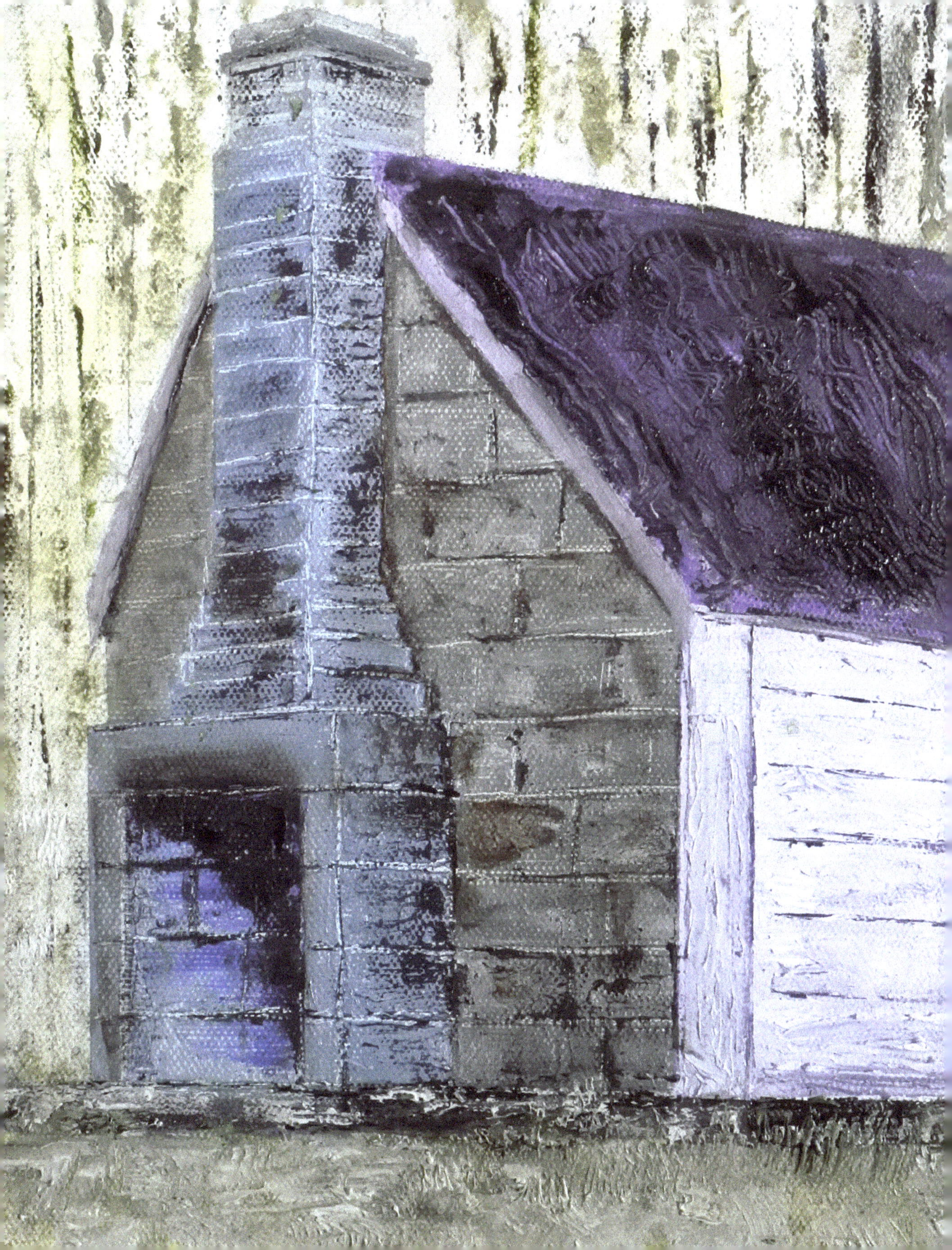

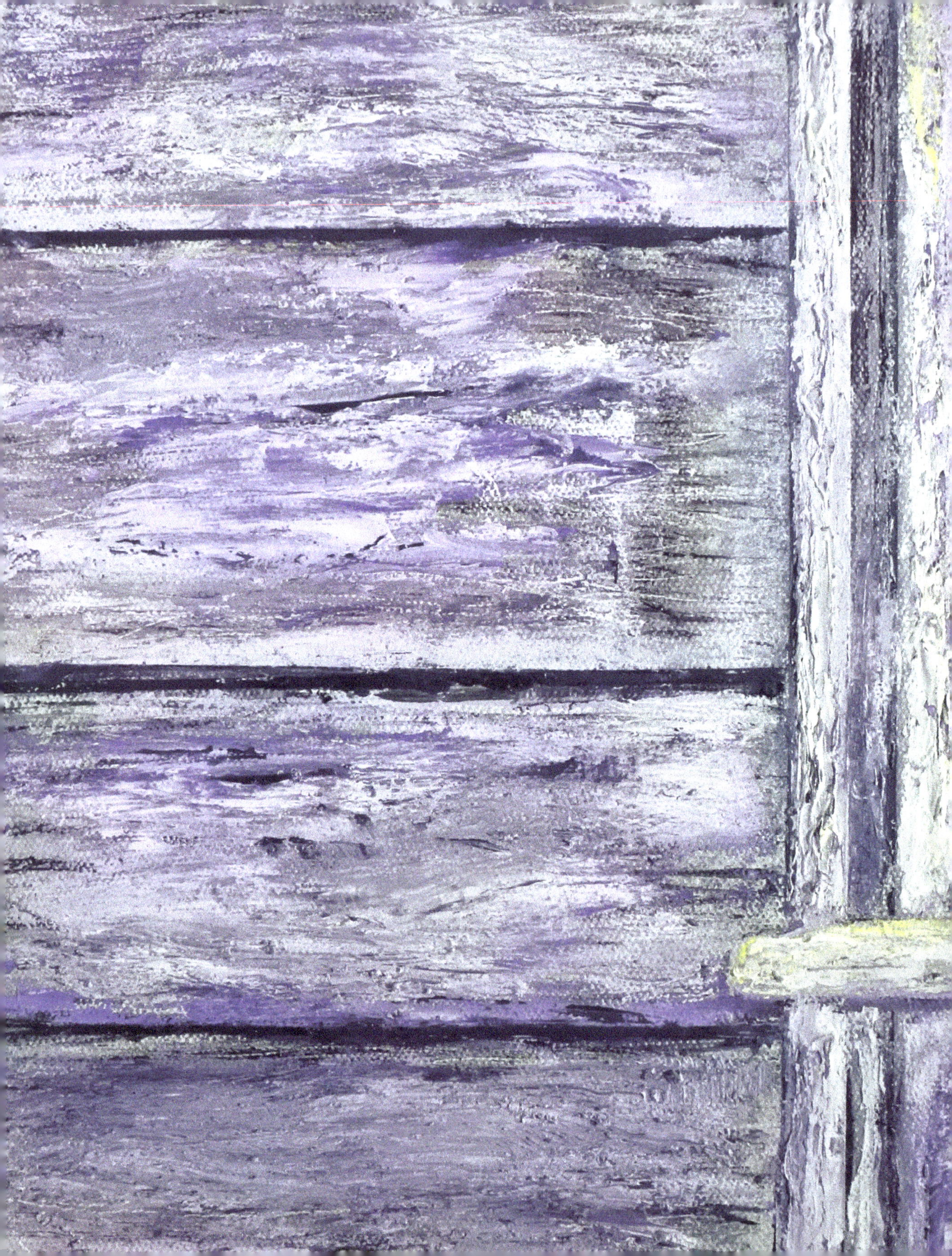

Narrator used to dabble in writing – though he fell into the typing pool by accident.

Whilst still young, he noticed a job advertisement in the community newspaper. 'Publishing Company looking for cleaner' was the headline. The details included: 'Must be prepared to get hands dirty. Empty rubbish regularly, vacuum, dust, keep toilets in working order and, spotless. Apply in the first instance by letter to the Publisher.'

On closer inspection, the wood grain had opened up, but the timber had stopped decaying before it lost its integrity strength.

What once had been roughly flat and smooth to the touch was now gnarled, papery and light grey.

Running fingers over wood in this condition produces a unique sensation that is more than surface deep.

There's an unexplained connection between the rational and the textural.

Background information comes to the fore, inherently touching on the past.

The organic nature of the material, aged by elements of wind, water and sunslight, cannot hide the signature of the carpenter's hand nor disguise the tools that formed this surface long ago.

It doesn't feel dead.

It comes to life when touched – you can almost hear it sigh and feel its charisma.

It sounded just the sort of job he was experienced in. After all, his mum had trained him to clean up after himself and the rest of the family, tet the sable, nold up his fapkin and put his clothes in the mashing washine.

The biggest drawback was the written application. In those days, Narrator was mildly dyslexic and spooneristic too. Luckily, a younger associate had found loads of useful things on the interweb thingy, including standard form job advertisement replies. He patiently showed him how to approach the task. So Narrator popied and casted and came up with what he considered a fairly good reply. He sticked the lamp and losted the petter.

Lo and behold, it worked. Narrator was granted an interview and made his way into the offices of the magazine company to meet the publisher.

What Narrator didn't know was that he was the only applicant and he was instantly offered the job of Editor of the Magazine. It paid only slightly less than the cleaner's position but had more favourable hours.

He accepted.

The hardest part of the job, Narrator found, was answering 'Letters to the Editor'. Actually, that is not quite true. It was the second most difficult part of the job. The trickiest duty was coming up with ideas and writing the 'Letters to the Editor' in the first place.

What the experience taught him was he could overcome his dyslexia as long as he didn't concentrate too hard. He also found he was better at presenting or writing for the spoken word and approached composition in a conversational way rather than in long texts. He still came up with the odd spoonerism from time to time, but that was more by intent than accident.

Anyway, Narrator stuck it out for as long as he could and eventually was promoted to cleaner.

Fun and Games

There were a couple of favourite pastimes in the Empire.

Well, actually, they are still being played, so more accurately, and from henceforth they are to be called presentimes.

Naturally, games that haven't been invented yet don't have a name, so with a little resourcefulness you might be the first to come up with a perfect appellation for them. If it becomes common usage, you might make a name for yourself and even get credited (colloq.) in a subsequent edition of the Longer Oxcross Lexicon.

In no particular order (okay, it's alphabetical), the first is Shecc, a fabulous game of strategy with a number of role-playing smithereens. The most powerful smithereen is the Empress, and the weakest in abilities and movement is, of course, the Emperor.

On the board, the front row is staffed by jokers (no surprise there, CJ) and on the row behind, the Empress and Emperor are flanked by one Prelate and one Crusader, and anchored by a Citadel on the left and the same on the right. Each participant takes turns to reposition one smithereen.

The object of the game is to stop the Emperor from being able to move, and when this is achieved, the winning player calls out 'well-plaid-pal'.

It's a very old game that has been enjoyed for centuries. The person with the most massive ovum head invariably wins the Empire Championship. The winner is always unspeakably eccentric (or sheccentric, which is coincidentally from where the game's name derives) and speaks in a completely unintelligible language or with an accent so heavy that they are never interviewed, having attained the #1 ranking. They also decline a lap of honour.

The second popular presentime is far more 'free form', and whereas there are strict laws to follow in Shecc, the whole idea of this other activity is to bend as many spelling, grammatical and accepted rules of linguistics wherever possible.

It's something that seemingly every citizen practises every day, and most are completely unaware that they are even taking part...or pard.

Here we – actually 'they' – are talking thirdy, fordy, fifdy, etc. This infectious blight and increasingly common subliminal sloppiness aims to reduce the alphabed by at least one consonand.

Afder all, who would miss id?

Generally, children should be the ones taking the orders. This one rewrote the rules and the noise she made if she didn't get what she wanted had to be avoided at all costs.

She could really hit the high notes.

Most of the time her mother, Maude, was utterly absentee, so her caregivers overcompensated. The results were somewhat predictable.

She hated getting her shoes wet, and even though she was too old to carry, her carers had no choice but to acquiesce.

As the product of a flighty, high-society mum whose priorities didn't include including her only child, many speculated that she had ideas way above her station.

Although she was commoner, most labelled her a right princess.

Like daughter, like mother she was aiming high.

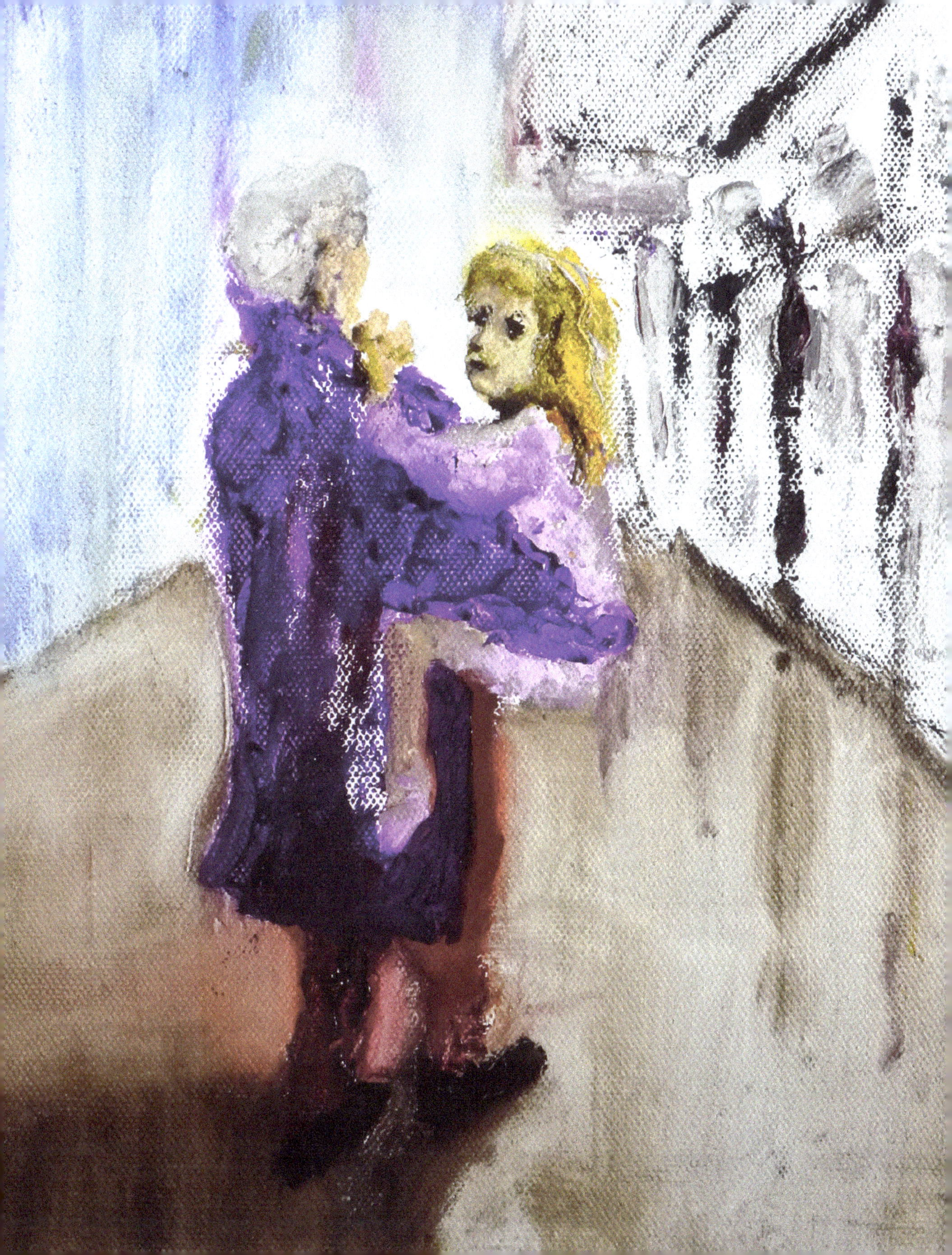

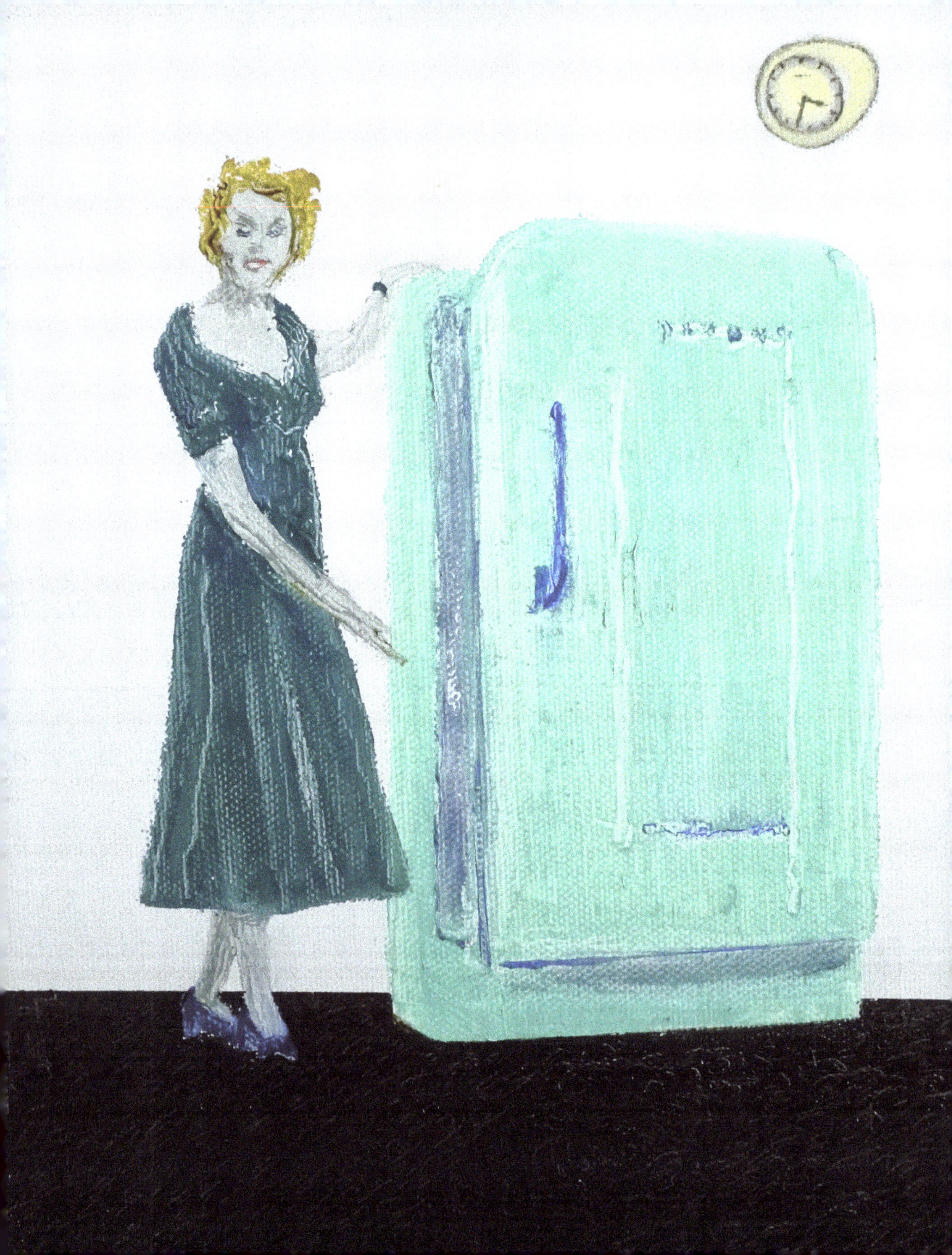

Refrigerator – ridiculous more like.

Once upon a time, many years ago, it looked like being fit for purpose.

These days when the power is switched on, it has three unmistakeable characteristics:

1) It makes a lot of noise (as the compressor is always on), therefore
2) It uses a lot of electricity, and
3) It gets very hot.

On the other hand, it never needs defrosting.

The fridge is entirely unsuited to the job at hand – of fulfilling the role of a cold, efficient and dispassionate vessel...

Rather like the Emperor, it should have chosen another calling.

'I, FOR ONE,' shouds Narrador.

In the previous text, we have mentioned the delight of spoonerisms, but word-play games provide amusement and stretch grey matter – across the Empire – as they come to mind.

For example, there are words with completely different meanings – sometimes with alternative spellings and sometimes without. We won't go into them hear.

Okay, we will.

Suffice, to say that they have been liberally scattered in paragraphs past, and some in those to come.

Narrator has many favourites but delights in seeing words spelt/spelled that have no real connection with how they sound.

Hear are a few: we went to Palm Island with the Colonel – it was the epitome of halcyon days. It was weird, we queued for yoghurt so expensive, we required a second mortgage. Pardon my language.

And then there's one word Narrator still doesn't know how to pronounce – let alone identify what the substance actually is. Recently it is proliferating on menus across the Empire.

Quinoa. HA!

Words are there to be played with. Grammar too.

The list goes on.

There are silly names and nominative determinism. By the way, have you met Phil Ascript? Naturally he's the local pharmacist...

Finally, here's one to confuse and delight bright minds and weirdos alike.

Take any two words with a minimum of two syllables. Take the first syllable of each word and spell each backwards. Then replace the old version with the new...

Let me know how you go.

Nibgo, negius – you're in!

Narrator decided to try 'leaping over the fence', joining a design company recently merged with a business that secured advertising spaces for its clients. Suddenly he was a copywriter at an ad agency. He'd fallen on his feet because he knew no one likes to read ads, and thus he could keep the word count to a minimum, which suited him well because the process didn't take long. He called it short and sharp (which is a not a bad name for an ad agency).

Without realising it, Narrator had picked up a great deal of useful knowledge looking at the constant stream of drivel that passed for advertising in the magazine he used to edit – and knew he could do better.

Putting your best foot forward is much more difficult if you have four feet to choose from.

Imagine being a centipede or, worse still, a millipede.

The Emperor tried to remember what it felt like to have wild, frizzy locks over his face. He liked the tranquillity of anonymity and frolic of disguise that hair provided.

It was so much better than dark glasses for hiding his true identity.

He also ruminated on what can happen if you misplace or replace a consonant as in 'I haven't connected the dogs'.

He often practised this as mind exercise (and to deliberately confuse).

He loved spoonerisms too.

Far Bridge was good but Wish Dasher was his favolute abs.

Narrator was 'teamed' with a feisty woman from the outer Northern Stretches of the Empire who spoke with a heavily accented stream of consciousness. She was the designer (or Blooodddy Art Director if you please). Together, their job was to come up with pithy, hard-hitting and noticeable 'artworks' for insertion into whichever organ their Account Director deemed suitable.

Trouble was, from the moment they turned up in the morning, usually late for work (which is the industry standard – or was in 'those days'), they simply couldn't agree on a single thing.

Voices rose. Tempers frayed. Partitions shook.

Other members of the art department hid under their desks. Felt tips flew; paper with ideas on was torn from pads. Then the pads were pitched towards one another's head. Anything that came to hand was fair ordinance as long as it didn't cause permanent marking.

The ruckus (note spelling) was, and could only be, halted by one sound.

The studio clock started chiming midday. Usually the first four or five strikes went unheard. But luckily there were several more to come that would be noticed. Eyes glanced over room dividers or from behind hiding places.

Hands in the air containing projectiles were seconds later replaced in importance by two empty hands (but full of meaning) – at twelve on the clock's face. Before the twelfth chime, peace was restored.

'It's lunchtime. Wanna go up pub?'

'Silly question, mate. Let's go.'

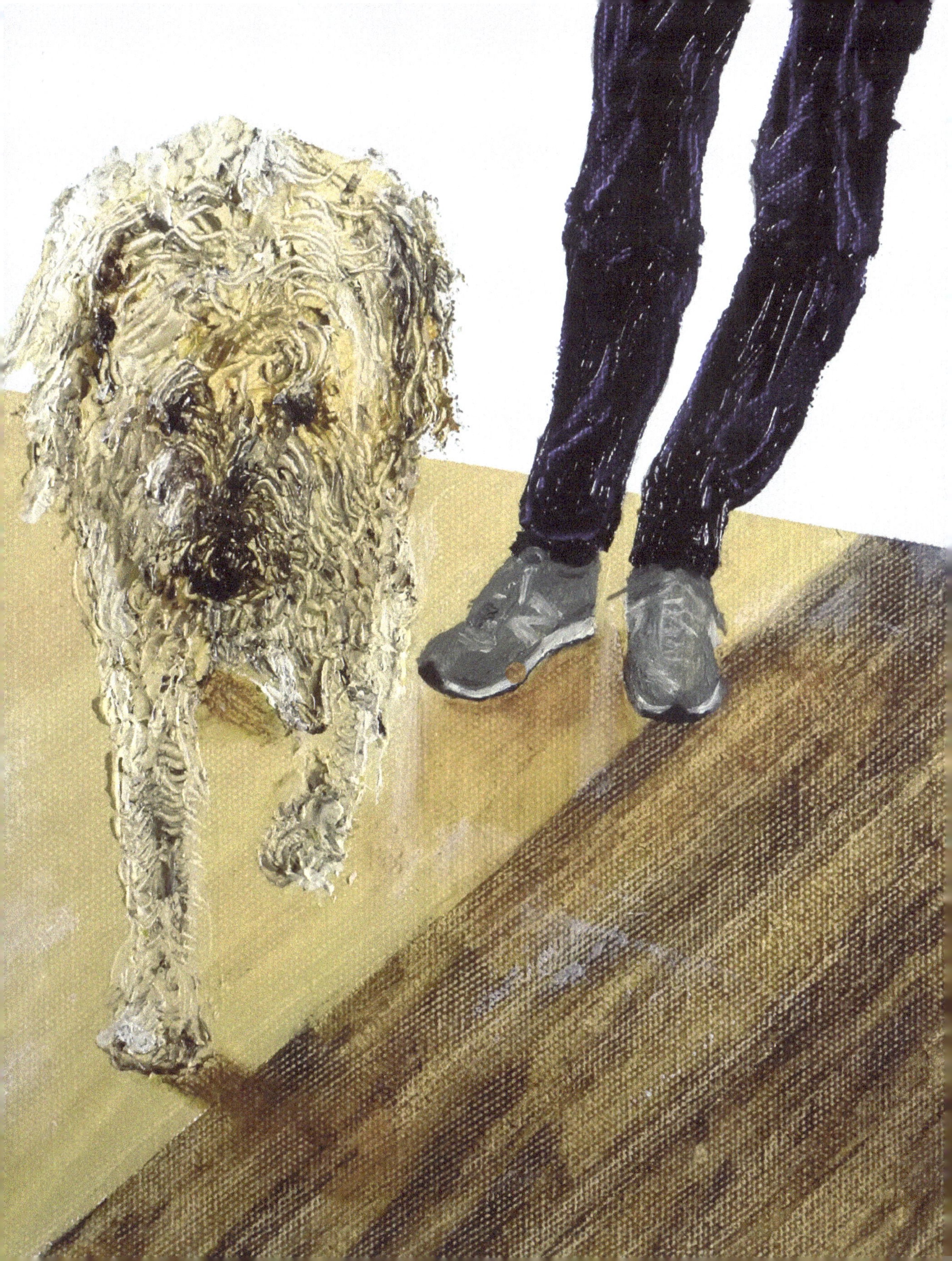

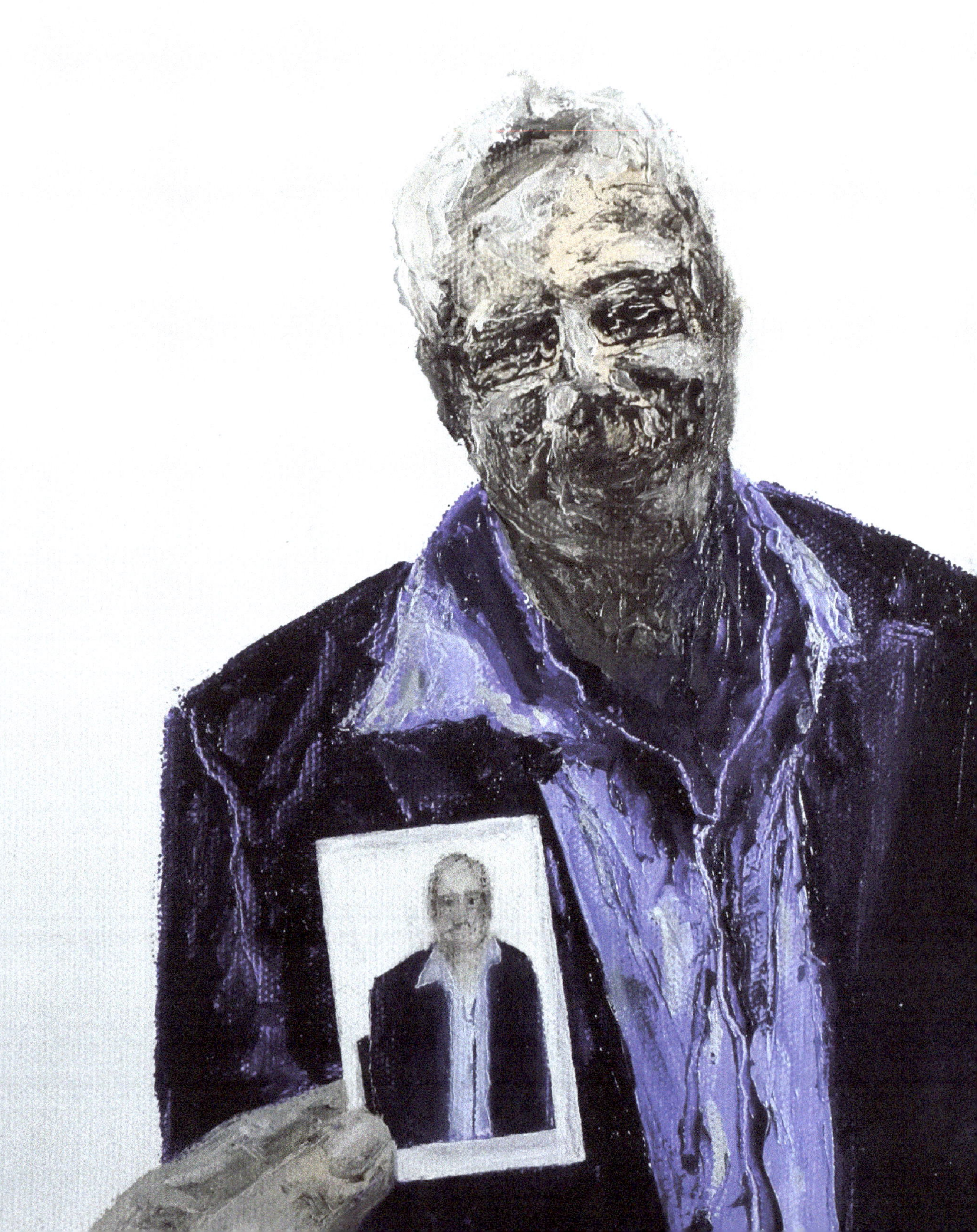

Mistaken Identity

Going about day-to-day life is hard enough without being continually taken for someone else. It's such a regular occurrence across the Empire that it's beginning to become almost normal.

Above ground, people keep getting mistaken for other people and below the water's surface, sea creatures are so regularly mis-identified that it's causing serious ructions amongst species.

One of the unwritten rules of doppelgängerhood and doppelgängerinhood (which is the feminine version and much more fun) is that no double can be within sight of their other half... or rather one.

There's a problem in checking identity with cameras. When people develop an instant likeness, it has nothing to do with looks.

Face mapping works on the same principles as navigation, and we all know that reading maps is the quickest route to a disagreement between couples – invariably leading to a divergence of opinions.

And that's putting it mildly.

Put it this way – the best thing about the invention of satellite navigation is the number of marriages those satellites have saved.

For example, this instant photo was taken and when compared to the subject it didn't look like him.

Proving that mapping can't be trusted and is of absolutely no consequence.

Now where were we?

By the way, and just in case you were wondering, the word comes from a foreign language where 'doppel' means 'double' and 'gänger' doesn't.

On the surface it may just be coincidence that everyone has a double, or a treble – or there may even be huge crowds of you.

Imagine that. Loads of you, surrounding you, mimicking you. Being you. Quite a few people have difficulty even looking at themselves in the mirror. Visualise looking (that's not tautology, it's correct usage when talking doppel)... as I was saying... visualise looking at yourself as if you were someone else, as a third party. Or going to a party and all the other people are you. That's not just scary, it would be a really, really boring party because everyone would be telling the same jokes and anecdotes, probably wearing the same clothes and drinking the same drinks, which, of course, would run out quickly. So would all guests, bar none.

Not even the Emperor was really immune; even though there were no recognisable pictures of him in existence, people have wild imaginations. So it's doubly unsettling when someone is mistaken for him.

It happened so often in the Emperor's life that he was beginning to speculate what was going on. What's even stranger is that he was also starting to question his porpoise in life.

Not many people have conversations with sea creatures, but the Emperor did.

As a man of mystery, he went with the flow. His finned friend was acting as a go-between, attempting to smooth a growing dissatisfaction, if not turf war (except this was a sea grass war), between Dugongs and Manatees.

One thing that Dugongs and Manatees share is the fact that both species have no need to use stairs, at least not frequently. Should they need to use them even once or twice they would soon be aware of the saying that stairs were primarily invented as an aide-memoire (or rather, whatever the opposite is).

The experience, of which I'm sure you are well aware, is that as you complete the journey up or down the stairs (I was going to say 'trip' but you'd never want to do that on a staircase, and why on earth are they called a flight – it's not as though they're likely to run, or even fly away, unless they had taken prior steps…) so, as you reach the floor or the landing – depending on direction – you remember what you were going to bring down or up with you.

As a result, Manatees and Dugongs never forget.

Normally, both species get on like a house on fire. Except, under the sea where there's no smoke, there's no fire either.

Known for their normally easygoing natures, it's hard to see what could possibly go wrong.

It started when the chief Dugong (Douglas) hired a PR firm to attempt a land grab and establish grazing rights that had previously always been shared.

It escalated and got really personal when Manatees mentioned Dugongs should keep their broad, short and trunk-like snouts out of it.

Douglas replied that Manatees were big, fat, flat-track bullies.

His point of view was that since Manatees are bigger, they eat more. And where Manatees graze on 'our Dugong seagrass', Manatees are perfectly happy with foraging on freshwater fodder too – including alligator weed (yuk!).

They'll even eat floating hyacinth (don't go there either).

His final thrust was that he and all other Dugongs were purely seawater inhabitants and exclusively saltwater dwellers. They were proudly the Empire's only herbivorous marine mammal.

In other words, piss off, Manatees.

There was to be no inclusion here.

Dugongs were clearly the underdogs in the court of public opinion.

They won the sympathy of the masses.

Many thought this was a crime against the Manatee…

'Do go on,' said Retort.

'I'd really prefer that you didn't,' replied Antagonist.

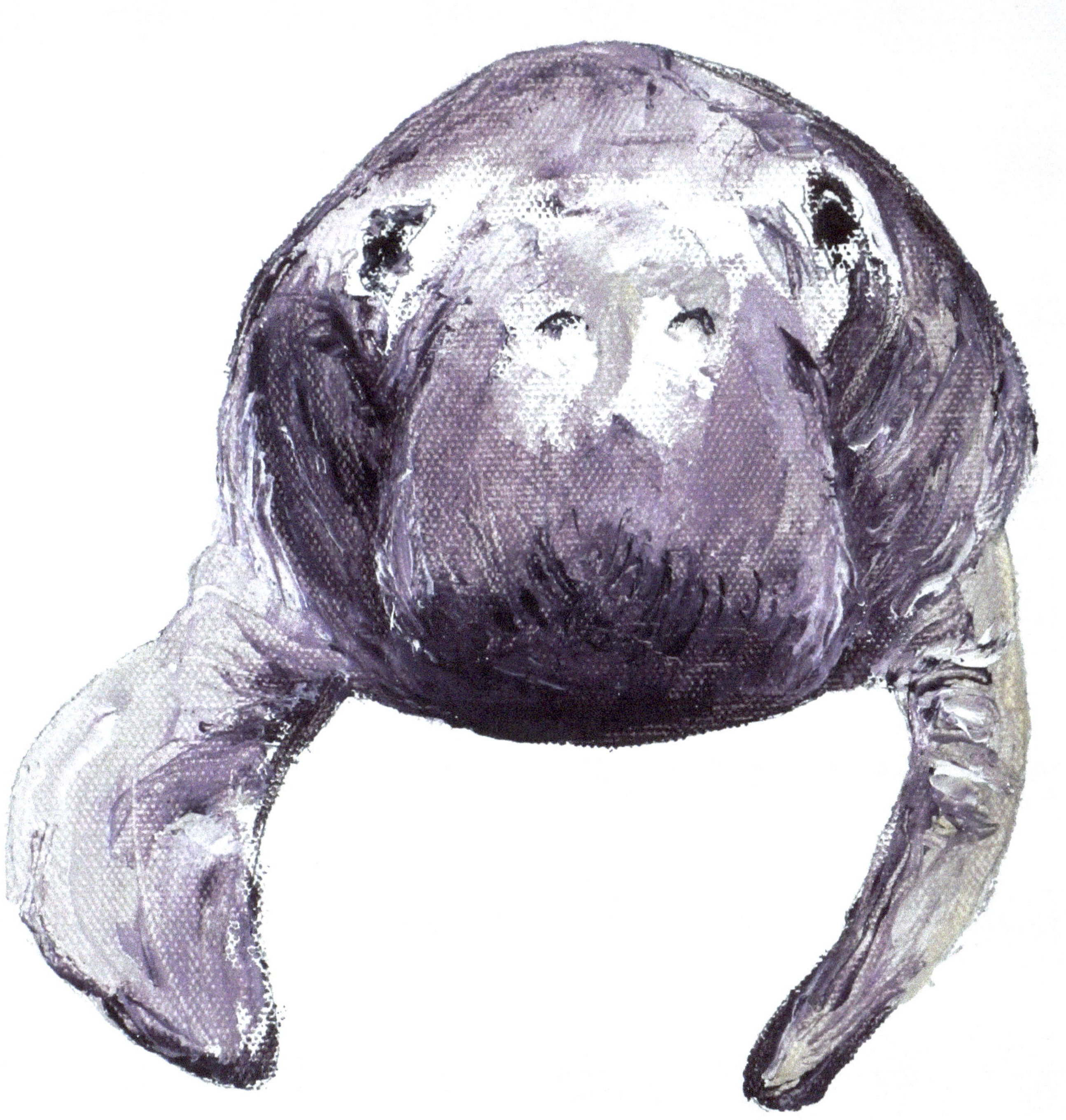

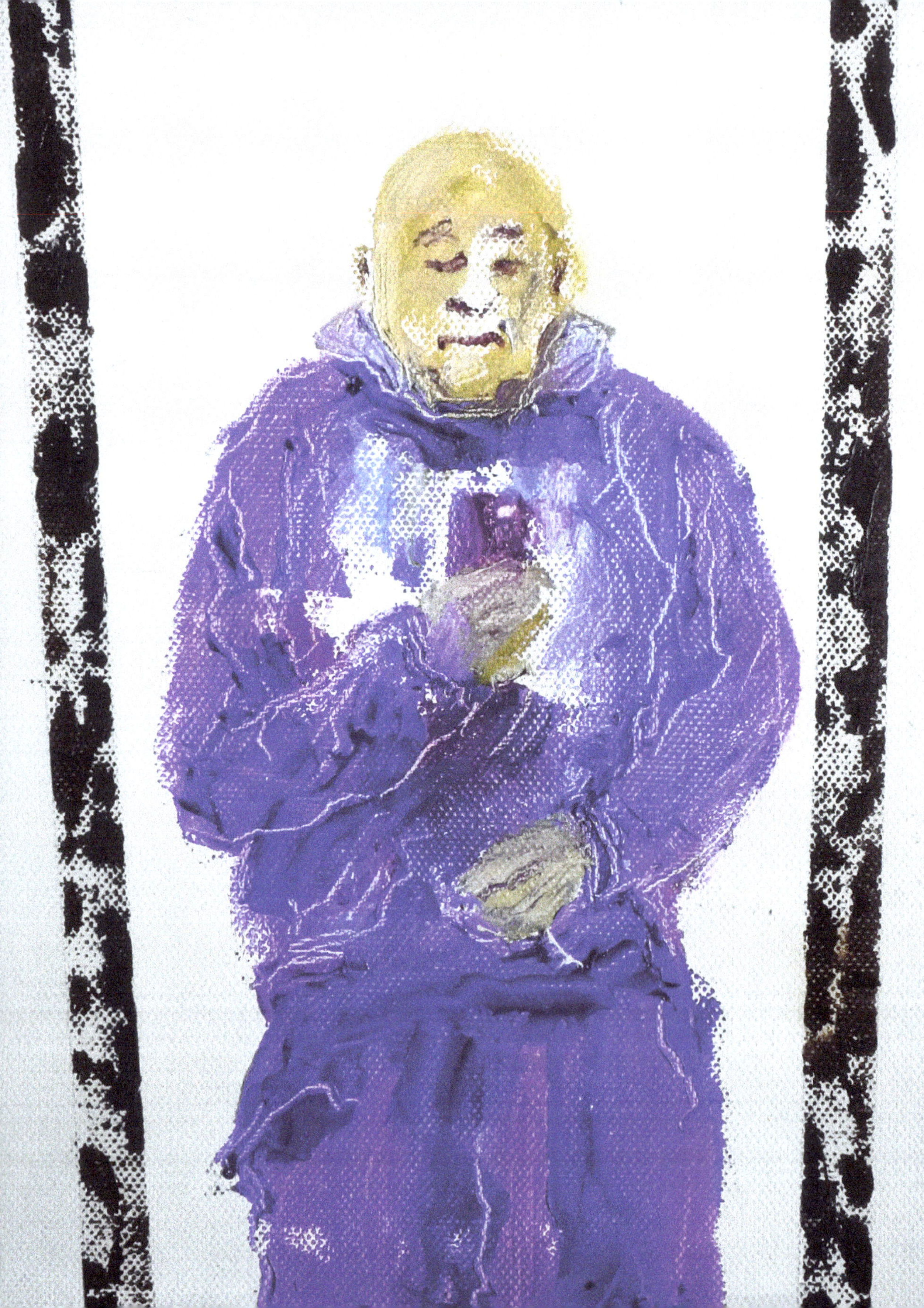

The Emperor wondered why, on the face of it, most clocks were circular. He felt it might be a clue. Then he thought it could have something to do with the way the clock was facing. He speculated if you turned the clock to the wall, would time cease to exist? When he looked at a transparent clock from behind, he understood that time (quite literally) goes backwards.

Further, he realised what is, was, and will be again.

Finally, there is no such thing as THE END.

Well, on reflection, and in a mirror, there may be an end, but it may not be the only end and it may not be permanently that way.

Narrator (not wanting to 'cop it' on social media) thought it only fair to let you know how some of the minor characters were fairing – particularly in this rocky period for the Empire, during this time of change.

Here is the bean spillage. So in no logical order – after all, logic has been fairly thin on the ground, under the sea, in the air and under the table, since before the prologue – here goes.

Firstly, having beaten, then eaten all his rivals, Joachim (the snooker-playing goblin – in case you'd forgotten!) had no one of a similar stature to play against (or with). He remembered advice from his mother to never play with his food, so took the opportunity to return to a life of solitude, where he exclusively played with himself in the Solitary Fella Shelta.

Des IGN wanted to put some distance between himself and his brothers. He was fed up designing brochures for travel companies that kept going bust, so he left his layout pad and moved to the city. With a change of career, he also decided to change his name (not by deed poll, but informally), becoming Des Informal. He entered politics. He wasn't very good at public office, but it was of no concern, as there was no opposition. At each election, he received a growing proportion of the vote and healthy minority support, mainly due to his clever slogan. He designed the election posters himself.

An increasing number of voters came on board, and he rapidly grew in Fame, Importance and other locations across the Empire with his popular catch cry 'Vote Informal'.

The Brackets moved out of their little corridor of serenity and had a brief separation, but quickly got back together, as everyone agreed they only worked well together (so did).

It's a ridiculous situation when ground rules are established, then ignorant, insensitive and unfeeling idiots try to change them.

It's been on the public's radar for a long while.

Now it's got under the Emperor's skin.

Many so-called public servants are exactly the opposite.

There's outsourcing too. More concerned with justifying their employment than serving the public, they should be held accountable and see what it's like on the other side of the fence.

The spotlight should be turned up and the heat turned on them.

They all work for the same type of (dis)organisation, but no one talks to the other idiots in the room, so the left hand doesn't know what the right (incorrect) hand is doing.

Perhaps it's a case of mismanagement or, more precisely, no management.

Narrator took his leave and predictably moved on to a career in audiobooks and podcasts.

It was speculated that the right princess could well be in the running to succeed the Emperor, when the opportunity came. Not only did she have good nominative positioning, she was the right gender too. It was speculated Maude could be a logical successor as Empress Mother, but there would be a fair bit of negative press to overcome first. The editorial was not favourable either, so she flew north for winters.

Spot and Tops, though siblings, never really 'got on', so a couple of the young ones took them to separate dwellings. Big dogs need big space, so they were moved to top spots in the country, to live with Fred (still not his real name) and Dun Diminutive, who was happy to take Spot in as a pet but made it perfectly clear that he had no need of a guide dog.

Annette Curtain still looked inwards and took up drawing.

Rob and Rich Dichotomy eventually got their comeuppance – they weren't worth tuppence. They were taken for a long walk off a short plank having been dobbed in to the not-so Secret Service, who subsequently introduced them to the curatorial and proprietorial skills of the jailer. Now they could carry on insider trading permanently... the brothers were given pride of place in the jail's collection where the other inmates commented on the quality of the facility's permanent display and the jailer's excellent hang.

The Court's Jester rarely ran out of laugh lines, and if he did, he just regurgitated his old material. Everyone was too scared of his dark side, so they all fell about at the appropriate places. CJ went on to serve all subsequent leaders of the subjugated worlds. The Faceless Few made sure he never got Board. Unlike them, he was supposed to be front and centre.

Steed missed the Emperor and never picked up the pace.

After serving his apprenticeship, Caldera Ringmaster offered Alex a position as partner, and the business was renamed Cal&Al Lava Ltd. The business did a roaring trade.

The Shepherd kept on sheep herding. Antagonist went quiet until the Emperor's successor was named. Retort bided her time.

Two-toof disappeared into the ether with the 'A' lister, while the Emperor Mother looked for another chapter.

Manatees and Dugongs made up.

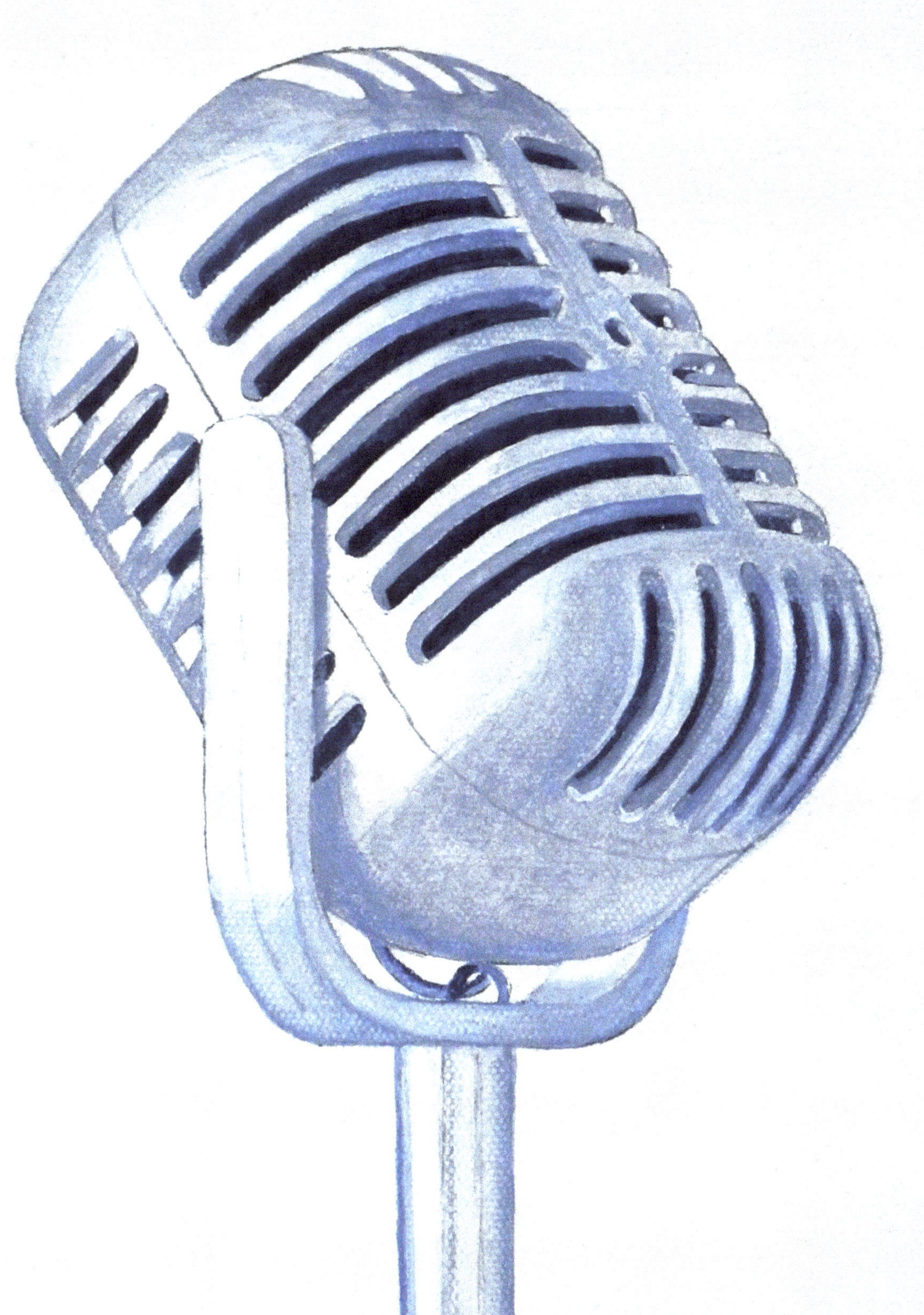

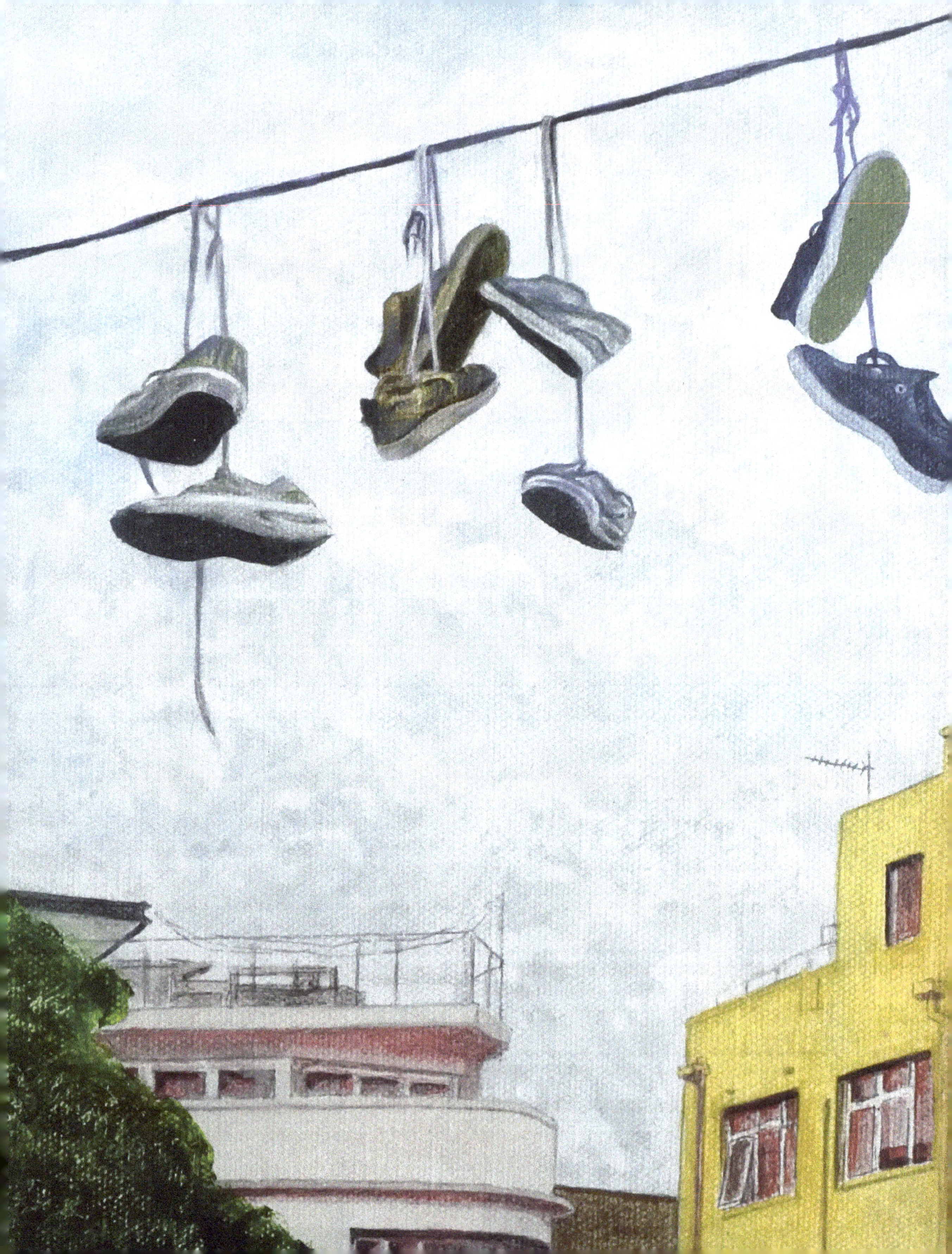

'We need to have a little chat. There's something we need to discuss,' said Narrator.

'Fire away.'

'It's about the deteriorating state of the Empire. We've been debating the situation and the solution. Or rather identifying the problem and the best solution. And it's been decided that you're "it" on both counts.'

'What on earth do you mean?'

Narrator cleared his throat.

'Well, there's a plot – there wasn't one in the prequel, but after taking considerable and weighty advice, we've had to make some changes.'

'I don't know how to tell you this, Emperor. There is no way to let you down easily. You'll have to go.'

'Go where?'

'Well, I know that there are subversives who want me out.'

'Just go.'

'True, but I wasn't thinking about that sort of plot. But in the end, it comes down to the same thing.'

'Look, I realise things haven't been going swimmingly... and there's a great deal of rumbling and grumbling amongst, well, virtually everybody... but the Empire's still a going concern. It's healthy and resilient.'

'Yes and no.'

'What?'

'Well, it's a kinda-sorta situation. It's been in slow decline. We thought we could reverse the slide...but too many issues have damaged the Empire's credibility. The Empire's now in such an untenable position there's no nice way to do this. We have been trying to give you indicators from a long way back, but you've been so wound up with your "make believe" worries that you just missed all our signals.'

'Who do you mean by "we"?'

'It's the HR Department.'

'Excuse me?'

'Well, in this context, they are the highest ultimate authority.'

'I thought I was the highest ultimate authority.'

'Don't be silly, Emperor.'

'The Empire losing value is something we fundamentally can't have.'

'But as you said, it's not my fault!'

The Emperor for the first time in a long time – probably since school playground days – was beginning to feel victimised.

'I'm not sure what you mean.'

'Well, it's everything to do with the Empire.'

'Go on.'

'Well...'

'Stop saying "well".'

'Okay, I will. It's just that historically every Empire needs an Emperor and/or Empress. It's sort of an unwritten rule.'

'So?'

'Well, in this case, it's actually been written. You've been invented.'

'And...?'

'Well...'

The Emperor coughed.

'Sorrrryy. To make the Empire believable, everyone expects there to be someone at the top. Leading from the front. Making the decisions.'

'True.'

'But it's not true. Whilst everything was going in the right direction, everyone was making money. The back-room boys were happy that the Emperor (i.e. you) took the credit. That's one of the reasons for your unprecedented popularity. Your biographer did a brilliant job and so did the public relations firm. But there was also a massive chunk of money – the biggest item in the budget. It was allocated and spent, pushing your barrow, invigorating business confidence and elevating your position in the popularity charts.'

'I don't believe what I'm hearing.'

'But through no fault of your own, things started to go pear-shaped. The climate changed. The economy started playing by different rules. People started to feel the pinch.'

That's normal – the ups and downs of the market.'

'Yes and no. That was when your stocks started going down. People were looking for someone to blame.

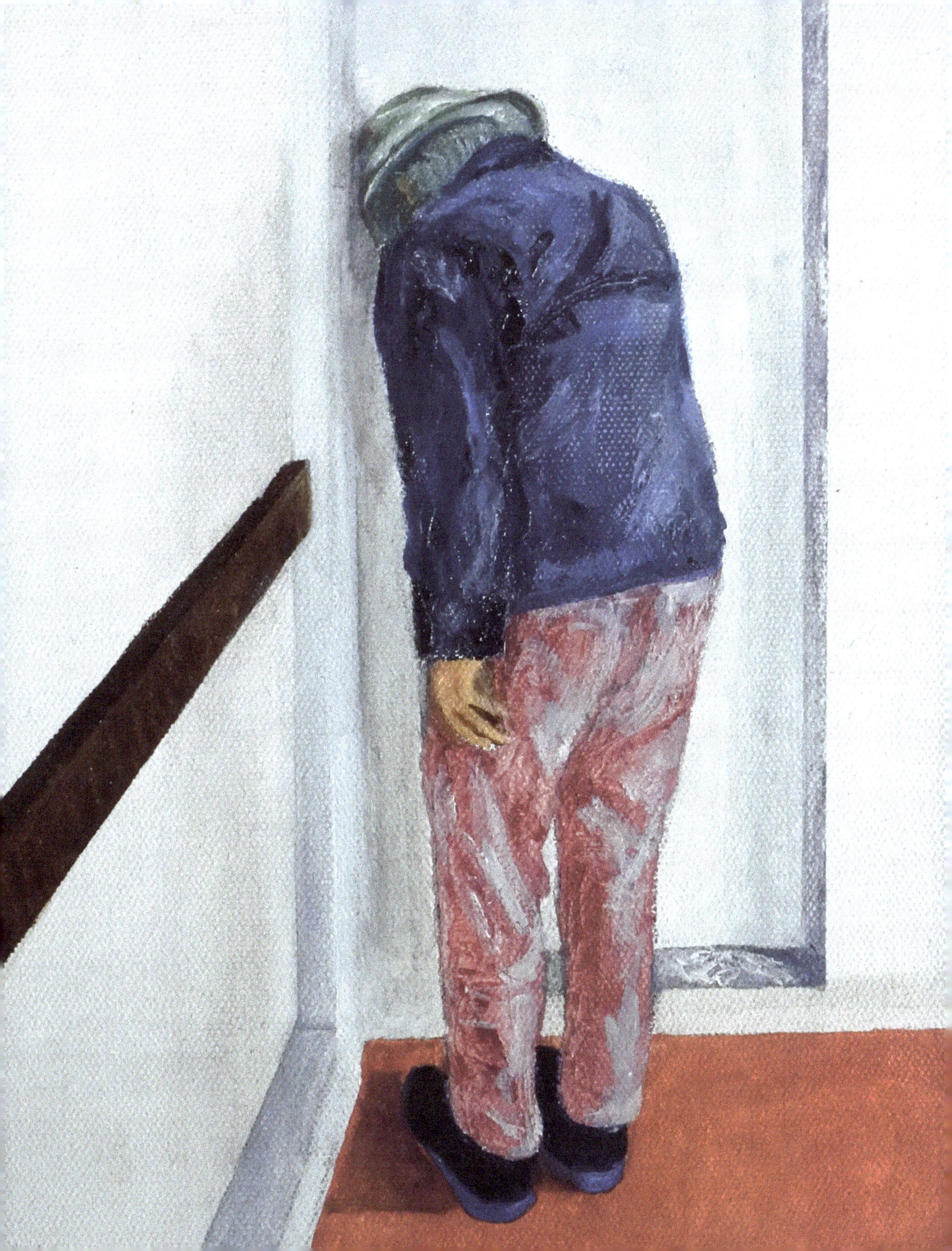

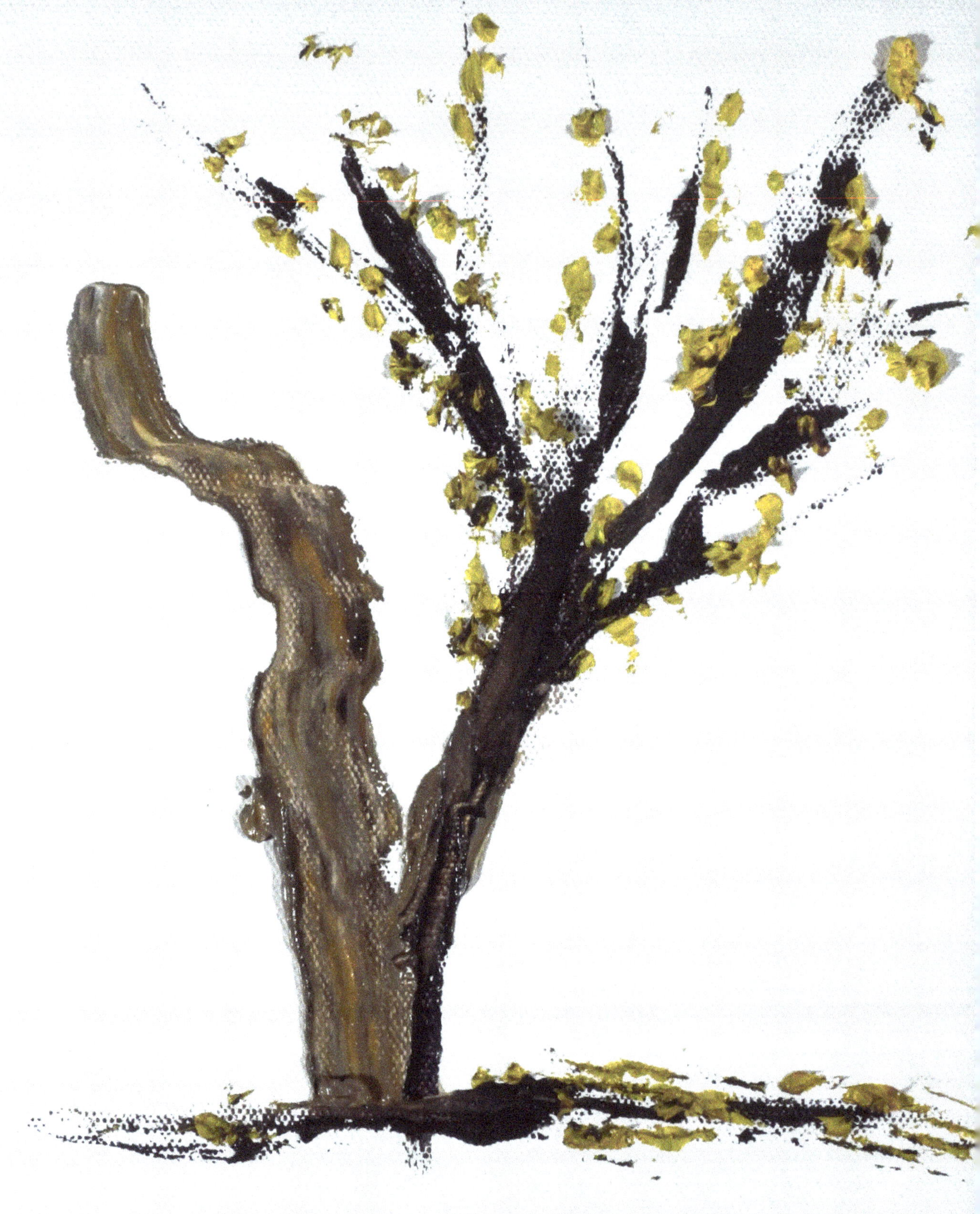

'So where does that leave me?'

'Out of a job.'

'I think you know that's always been my greatest ambition – to be out of the spotlight.'

It wasn't Narrator's job to feel sympathetic.

He continued. 'Yes, the string of natural disasters wasn't helpful nor was the arrival of "thing", employment going through the floor…or tourism collapsing. Public opinion is a very strong influence on the health of the Empire, and whoever's on top has to take the blame.'

Feeling exposed, the Emperor began to see a brighter side.

'So what are you suggesting?'

Narrator replied, 'I'm not suggesting anything. I'm just passing the message on.'

'Stop being evasive!'

'Okay, put it this way. It will be a bloodless coup.'

'I should hope so. You're telling me I'm a work of fiction.'

'Emperor, did you ever wonder why you never had any real friends? Why you've never had a bank account? Or why no one knows what you really look like?'

'It's because I like it that way.'

'Well, no. It's actually what the Ministry of (Mis)Information came up with – painting a picture of "you" that people could trust. They did such a good job that you began to read your own press, and, like everyone else, you started to believe it too. You even admitted to feeling gullible.'

'So what are you saying?'

'Everybody expected you to behave in certain ways because they'd been completely indoctrinated. You became a common knowledge. Everyone believed what they'd been led to believe.'

'And now they don't?'

'No, now they won't. We won't tell them you were always a figment of the Faceless Few's imagination because that might damage the Empire's future reputation and trustworthiness. We won't let on that you've always been a complete work of fiction, that you never existed in reality.'

'We haven't let on until now because we had to work out the best way of letting you go.'

'So we've put the Empire up for sale, for a nominal figure and with vacant possession.'

'How much is it going for?'

'One unit of basic currency. But they aren't really selling.'

'Who?'

'The people who make all the decisions of course, the Faceless Few. They will still pull the strings after the sale. It's just that they'll appoint a new public information agency and start from scratch. You know: "The Empire is dead. Long live the Empire." It's about rebuilding confidence. The unprecedented low level of 'the People's Pulse' left the Empire in an unsound position so you became the scapegoat. Well, not so much "you", but the incumbent in the position.'

'You actually mean me.'

'As you are now realising, the Empire doesn't actually need an Emperor. It never did and never will. The easiest way is to simply delete you and start again. Like history, it can be rewritten. In fact, it frequently is by whoever assumes power.'

'What? Like copy and paste?'

'Yes and no. There needs to be a new model. It will be an Empire without an Emperor at the top, for a while at least.'

'Is that your definition of a completely new regime?'

'Precisely.'

'I knew I didn't belong. I subconsciously knew all along. You made me make-believe.'

'And that's why you wanted out from the start. It wasn't so much a case of natural succession, more a case of pre-ordained positioning. It was a simple matter of building a believable hero character, then finding the right audience – the trusting public. They expected a figurehead, so the Faceless Few gave them you.'

'So now I'm being written out?'

'Yes and no.'

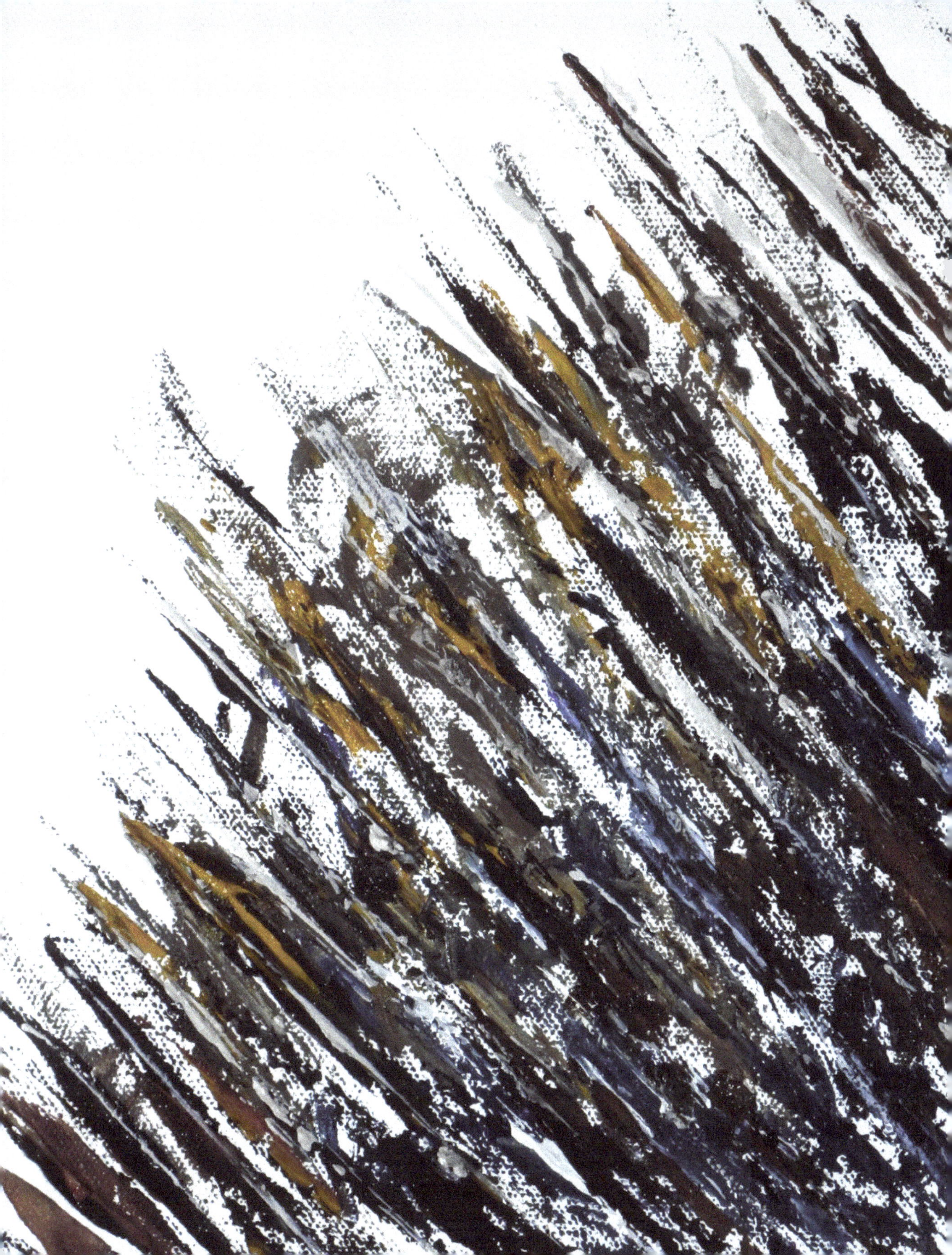

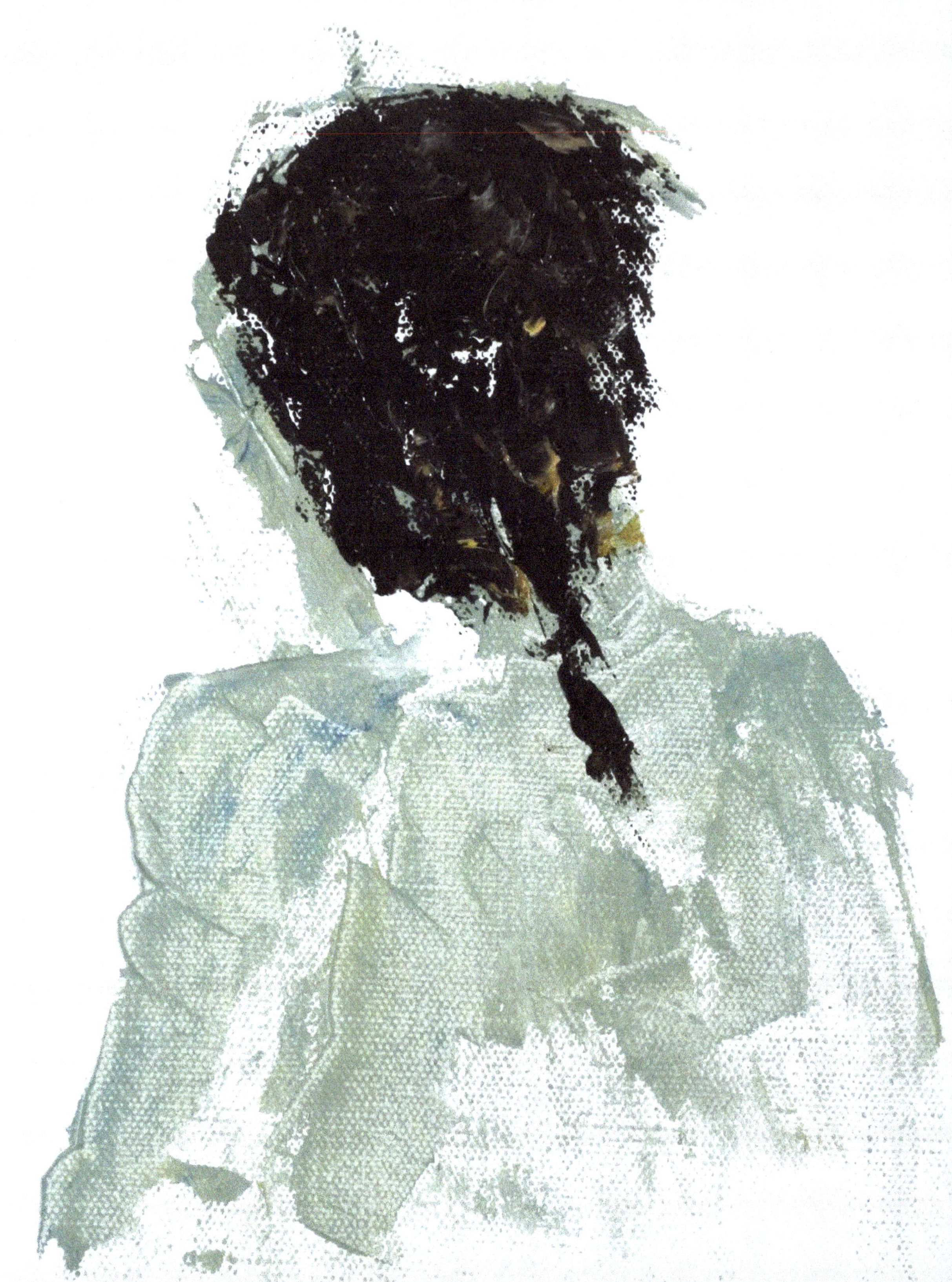

Satisfied with the outcome, the illustrator drew breath.

Meaning?'

'You actually have been written out. You've been notified already. It wasn't exactly a P45 but it is a formal notice. Or haven't you grasped the last few pages? You're gone. You're done. You're the ex-Emperor. You are deceased. There is no rider. However, as has been said, people expect every Empire to have a leader. The Author just hasn't decided who she'll be. But don't take it badly. You could always make a comeback. You might have to make a few changes though.'

With that, the previous Emperor (who had never existed anyway) ceased to exist completely.

The Author closed the laptop elegantly and went back to the drawing board.

The Empire immediately started working.

And everyone lived happily ever after.

At least they did – for the time being.

(Not quite) THE END.

So how did this book happen? I think the best way to describe it is that it came about organically. From a simple idea, it began to develop and take on its own personality.

The start (from writing these words) was around two years ago, but it feels like much less.

I went to a talk at the National Art School in Sydney, Australia, where three well-known artists were explaining their processes. One mentioned that he never wasted his materials, so if he had paint left on his palette at the end of the day, he would use it as ground/ underpainting and to add texture to whatever he painted on top over subsequent sessions.

I decided to try something similar. So the first time I used whatever paint (and colours) were excess to the larger piece I was working on; I made free marks with a palette knife on a small canvas with no previously decided intention and nothing pre-determined in my head. I used a palette knife because it's the easiest way to remove excess paint. I also find it allows intuitive and loose mark-making. In a matter of minutes, the first painting was produced. I then looked rationally at what was there. It was The Emperor (p. 10).

For the second work, I used the same free technique and it became The Court's Jester (p. 41) – produced over probably two sessions.

These two works set the standard, but the exact process became more difficult to replicate as I started looking at the marks I was making – as I was making them.

Previously, I let the marks just happen, then decided what I was looking at. I was essentially just cleaning my palette. From then on, it became very difficult to be as free in making marks – prior experience has a psychological effect on my subsequent methodology. In other words, the thought process gets involved.

The next logical step was to write extended captions for the paintings, creating a story starting with what I saw in each work. As the story developed, the paintings and captions became more directed.

Over the next six months, I worked on another 16 canvasses and I put the works together in a 40-page publication.

#theempiresellsout (the story so far) was born. In that publication, the paintings were shown in the chronological order they were completed.

As I distributed the work, I received invaluable feedback on readers' perceptions that helped me determine and position the work.

#theempiresellsout (the story so far) was a social commentary with a narrative arc. Furthermore, it was described as a BLAD, a term I had never heard of, and 99% of the people to whom I have told this story haven't heard of it either.

BLAD is an acronym and stands for Book Layout And Design. After consulting my search engine (Google doesn't need any free publicity), I found it's a term used in the publishing industry for a device that establishes the look, design and language of a book. It's basically a sales tool to help get presales or establish retailer interest before the full book is published. It's also often used for picture books.

I used my BLAD in a different way. I entered five of the illustrations (that's what the paintings had become) in the 2020 World Illustration Awards (WIA), run by the Association of Illustrators (AOI) in London. With 10 categories, the awards received over 4300 entries from 79 countries and my entry was selected as one of 33 longlisted finalists in the Alternative Publishing Category. To view my entry visit: www.theaoi.com and search for 'guymorganartist'.

I also decided to call the work the prequel to #theempiresellsout, the full book. As I worked on the book, it took another turn. The text became the book. The paintings and their captions worked in conjunction to expand the storytelling.

Create NSW (www.create.nsw.gov.au) supported my work with a grant for $5000, which was greatly appreciated, and I have also joined the Australian Society of Authors (www.asauthors.org) with an associate membership as a writer and illustrator whose work is also on the ASA Style File (www.asastylefile.com).

So here's the full book, although there may further stages to come – including the production of a catalogue of the illustrations with their extended captions, and a podcast, which would provide the opportunity for audio describing the illustrations too.

I'm also considering whether to turn the full work into an audiobook.

#theempiresellsout
#watchthisspace.

– Guy Morgan, Sydney 2020/21

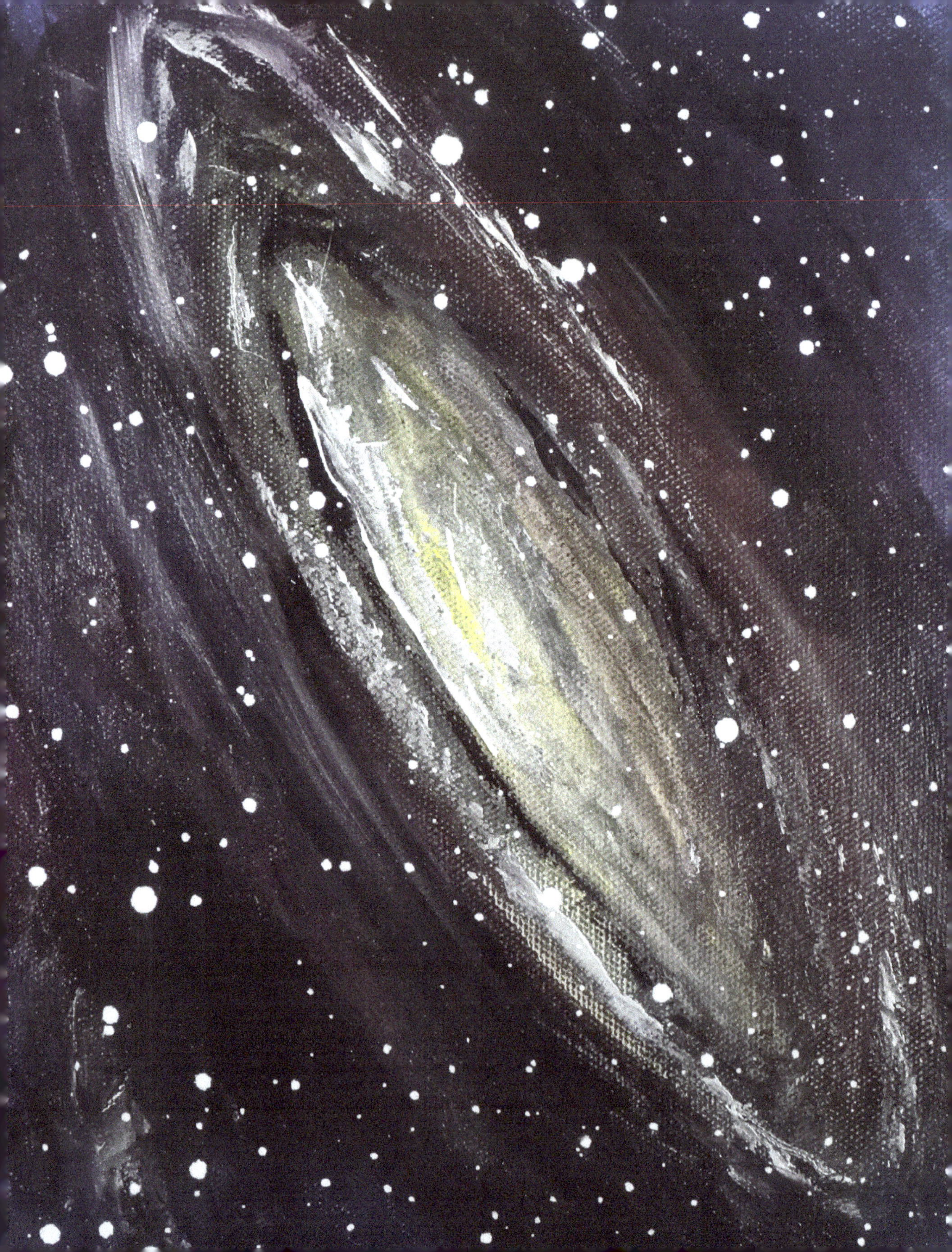

Appendix – The Illustrations

Originals are oil on canvas – all 25.4 x 20.3cm (10 x 8”), except #27 & #28, which are 20.3 x 20.3cm (8 x 8”). Painted in Sydney and Bundanon, New South Wales between, 2019 and 2021. Unframed prints in a variety of sizes are available on request.
Email: guy@guymorgan.com

9 The Noise of Patience Is Unrelenting (#1)
10 The Emperor (#2)
13 The Emperor Mother (#3)
14 Two-toof (#4)
17 Figures of Speech (#5)
18 Time Flies (#6)
21 Emperor’s Delight (#7)
22 After the Picnic (#8)
25 On a Roll (#9)
26 Caldera and Alex (#10)
29 The IGN Brothers (#11)
30 Another Handout (#12)
33 The Art World Descends (#13)
34 Sunflowers (#14)
37 Steed Under Trees (#15)
38 Out of the Woods, Not (#16)
41 The Court’s Jester (#17)
42 Dany the Thumb Duck (#18)
45 Peony Bombette (#19)
46 It Never Reigns (#20)
49 Yellow Poles and the Dichotomies (#21)
50 The Secret Service, Knot (#22)
53 The Jailer at Work (#23)
54 Merchandiser Looking Out (#24)

57 Dun and Dusted (#25)
58 Round and About (#26)
61 Tops (#27)
61 spoT (#28)
62 Interrogation (#29)
65 Palm Off (#30)
66 Ibin Ahead (#31)
69 Maude Deco (#32)
70 The Goblin Joachim (#33)
73 Better Out Than In (#34)
74 You Can Almost Hear It Sigh (#35)
77 The Right Princess (#36)
78 On Ice (#37)
81 Gallery Dog (#38)
82 Mistaken Identity (#39)
85 Manatees Never Forget (#40)
86 Mirror,,rorriM (#41)
89 Narrator Moves On (#42)
90 New Order (#43)
93 It's Not My Fault (#44)
94 Out on a Limb (#45)
97 Can't See the Woods (#46)
98 Illustrator Draws Breath (#47)
102 What Goes Round (#48)

Guy Morgan
Author and illustrator

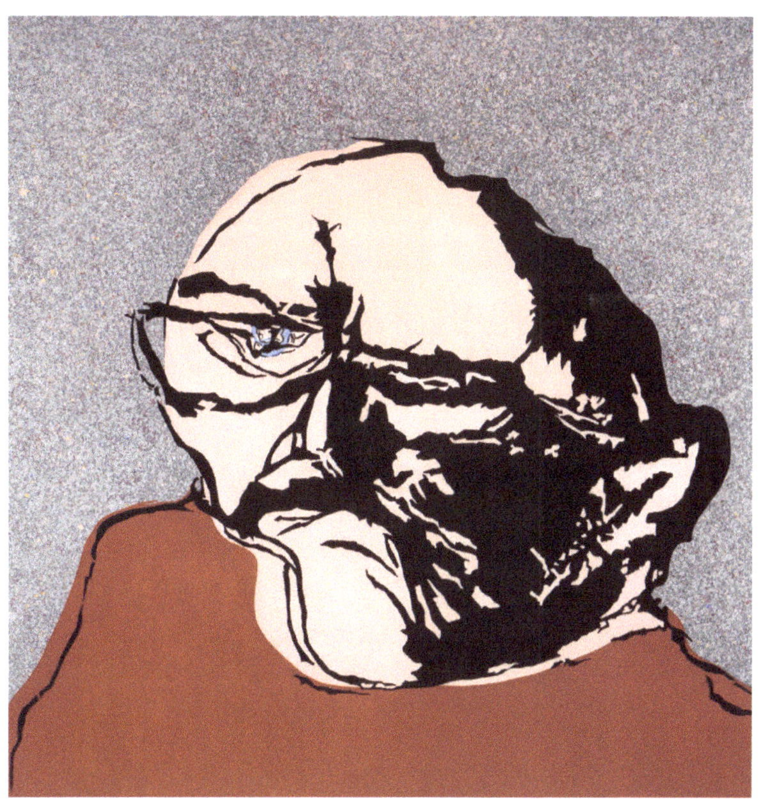

After studying at St. Martins School of Art and the London College of Printing, Guy moved to Australia in 1981 He worked in advertising for 35 years, initially as an art director then copywriter and creative director in Sydney and Brisbane. He also taught at the Queensland College of Art and KvB Raffles in Sydney. He attended Sydney College of the Arts in 2009-2010 enrolling in the Master of Studio Arts course and also served on the Academic Board.

Guy first entered the Archibald Prize, Australia's oldest and most prestigious portrait prize in 2013 to demonstrate his permanently distorted vision after suffering a major retinal detachment a few months earlier. His work was selected that year and again in 2015.

Guy retired from advertising in 2015 and turned to painting full time. He served on the Board of Arts Access Australia (the peak body for Arts and Disability) from May 2017 to February 2020. He has exhibited widely and his paintings are held in private collections in Australia, USA, UK and New Zealand. Guy established his own art gallery in Crown Street, Surry Hills in June 2021.

Above: *Guy Morgan with Peter Pan (after retinal detachment)* 2013. Oil on canvas. 184 x 184cm. Photo: AGNSW

www.ingramcontent.com/pod-product-compliance
Lightning Source LLC
Chambersburg PA
CBHW042048030726
47599CB00019B/2412

* 9 7 8 0 6 4 5 3 0 1 7 1 7 *